Honey,

MAKE A DIFFF

Go
EriC

# THE DNA OF BUSINESS
## FOR NETWORK MARKETING

## ERIC GOLDEN

Published by

Now You Know Press

In association with

Carpenter's Son Publishing

The DNA of Business for Network Marketing:  A Model for Success

© 2013 by Eric Golden

Published by
Now You Know Press
12305 SE 55th Ave Road
Belleview, Florida 34420

In association with
Carpenter's Son Publishing
Franklin, Tennessee

Interior Design by Suzanne Lawing

Edited by Lorraine Bossé-Smith

978-0-9889403-2-1 Trade Paperback
978-0-9893722-2-0 Hardcover

Printed in the United States of America

www.theDNAofBusiness.com

# Contents

## SECTION 3—IMPROVEMENT AND RESULTS

# Acknowledgements

THIS BOOK WAS MADE possible because of a great group of people I have come to know in my personal and professional life. Each and every one of them has become friends, and most of them, even after many years, continue to regularly bless me with their honesty.

I owe my deepest gratitude to Scott and Jane Golden and Mark and Sheila Bernstein. You both knew me long before I had the knowledge or expertise to write this book but cared about me anyway.

Thank you, Linda Rose, my hiking and dining buddy. During the countless hours we spent discussing my ideas for writing The DNA of Business, you never once became weary of the journey, nor passive toward the destination. This book would never have been written if not for you.

To my business partners, Ryan and Jenny Chamberlin, I thank you for pursuing the relationship. Clearly, I was the one who benefitted most from knowing you. Your integrity and humility have remained steadfast throughout your young adult years, and I am excited about where your life is headed as you continue to impact others— the way you have me.

I owe a great deal to Gary and Gloria Horstmann, Gerry and Sharon Betterman, and Van and Irene Davis. I met you all professionally decades ago, and although we no longer are business associates, you're always available and always encouraging.

To my adopted brothers, Jeff Bolf, Troy Brown, and Byron Schrag, you have taught me the truest meaning of acceptance. Thank you.

To my colleagues, John Terhune, Korey Johnson, Ron Golz, Ralph "Bubba" Pratt, Malcolm Alexander, and Robert "Bo" Short, you make me want to be more than I am, while oddly never making me feel as if I haven't made something of myself already.

To Tim Foley, Terry and Yvonne McEwen, and Jim and Joyce Mercon, as the guiding forces early in my networking career, this book stems from the building blocks you have taught me.

To my new friends Dave and Abby Baird, thank you for opening your home, your car, and your city to me. You taught me how being inquisitive doesn't always have to come with a motive.

# Introduction

*"No problem can be solved from the same level that created it."*

\- Albert Einstein

DNA IS EVERYWHERE. What made Albert Einstein different from Charlie Brown? One was a brilliant scientist, and the other was a boy in a cartoon, who had a secret crush on a girl and hated school (wait—that sounds like every boy). What exactly differentiated them was DNA. Einstein had it; Chuck didn't.

Scientists figured out *Otzi*, a mummy found frozen in the Austrian-Italian Alps, is over 5,000 years old.[1] My question is, "How did they figure that out?" The answer: DNA.

Thomas Jefferson, Steve Jobs, Eddie Murphy, Paul McCartney, and even Justin Bieber, have all addressed fatherhood issues through DNA tests. Turn on any cop show, and some detective is grabbing a used wine glass, looking for a spot of blood or collecting a lose strand of hair.

According to DNA testing, Ted Bundy was guilty, and O.J. Simpson was not. DNA really is everywhere; we can't get away from it. DNA is who we are, where we have been, and has *everything* to do with where we are going. This is where I come in. If everything has some sort of *pattern*, then why shouldn't business have DNA?

As a multi-million dollar earner in network marketing, I

have invested close to thirty years in coaching and consulting with hundreds of the top income earners in the industry. Although noticeable differences exist between each of these individuals, I have come to understand their *similarities* make them successful. These traits were innate in some cases, while others had to develop them. But, they all arrived at the finish line with a commonality, which was not common at all. It was a type of Business DNA.

I am not the inventor of this DNA. I won't even claim to be the first to discover it. I am merely someone who has verbally shared my findings with over one-million marketers around the world and has now decided to write it in book form—for you.

The elements making up the DNA of Business would be the same no matter the industry. For this book, I have chosen to use verbiage, viewpoints, and background material from a network marketing perspective. I do this to pay homage to the industry that provided me the basis for understanding it in the first place.

Einstein defined insanity as "doing the same thing, over and over, and expecting different Results."[2] I call it reality. We need to change our habits so when we get to heaven, we never have to hear Einstein say, "I told you so!"

Network marketers are good at asking themselves questions. Is it worth it? What are people going to think? Will it work for me? Where will I find the time? Questioning isn't our problem. The dilemma is, no one is sure of the answers! This book will answer the most vital questions you need in order to have a successful business. I know this because I have used the DNA of Business (DNA-*b*) model for myself, and it worked.

I am a firm believer that most things can be explained scientifically. Who we are, what we look like, and how we behave has much to do with our genetic makeup. This means we also bring natural thoughts and reactions to the business world. These thoughts and reactions create a basis for every decision, every Dream, and every defeat. Left unattended, we will not deliver *what we want*—our DNA will deliver *what we are programmed* to receive. Do you want more? You need to change the program. You may not need to be *more*, but you will need to be *different*. The person you are today has delivered what you have today. If you want to change what you *have*, you have to change who you *are* or what you *do*. I can promise the DNA of Business (DNA-*b*) can provide you a model for doing this. It will not only provide you hope, but it can become your road map for developing the sustainable, life-long, residual, network marketing income you have targeted.

Amazingly, human DNA consists of about three billion base pairs (the structure of guanine and cytosine, or adenine and thymine, which defines life itself), and more than 99 percent of these bases are the same in each and every one of us.[3] This means less than one percent of this structure creates all of our differences. The 99 percent says we all want more, we all have fears, and we all are in need of some changes. The one percent differentiates our Dreams, Belief, and Results. Fortunately for you, the DNA-*b* is a model to change these differences into achieving the Results you are looking for. Regardless of how you're designed, what matters is *what you do* with that design. This may be a new concept to you, but I believe I can show you how fortifying specific personal elements will put you on the right track.

The basic premise is as simple as it is Urgent. Everything you do in life is part of some larger system. In order to maximize the experience, follow a formula or some type of model. If you know the formula or implement the model, you open the door to endless possibilities. The DNA-*b* acts as a working model that collaborates within any industry or company. It will produce Results for anyone, anywhere, anytime—if you use it to guide your efforts. With this said, no one ever reaches and sustains a level of success beyond his or her makeup. Therefore, looking at your personal DNA is imperative. Comparing the DNA of the person you are today against a model of the DNA you need in business will provide a clear understanding of the areas needing attention.

These life-changing principles will make a difference in your business, home, relationships, and life. *The DNA of Business for Network Marketing* will revolutionize your thinking, inspire change, empower momentum, and create the Dream life you've been looking for.

## CHAPTER ZERO

# What's the Big Deal?

*"The obscure we see eventually.*
*The completely obvious, it seems takes longer."*

- Edward R. Murrow

I DECIDED TO START with chapter "zero" because it is truly where your business begins—at zero. You may think you begin a network marketing business the day you sign an application, but this in no way represents what is really happening. You bring with you a whole bunch of things on your journey in this industry. You already have things you want, things you believe, things you are afraid of, things you will do, things you won't do, things you will go to, things you won't go to, things you will say, and things you won't say. See what I mean?

Although a million different things concern you, the problems you have building your business will always boil down to this: You are working too hard and thinking too much! I don't expect you to believe this yet, but I assure you this will become evident somewhere in these pages.

To help frame your mind and make reading this book easier, I will tell you the secret right here in chapter zero—a chapter that isn't even supposed to be in a book! This isn't the secret of life, but it is the secret of surviving life in the network marketing industry.

Here it is: *Make your phone calls!*

Almost every minute and every dollar you spend on books, conference calls, videos, trainings, conventions, counseling, and, for sure, when you meet your upline for coffee, will relate to this crucial statement: make your phone calls. Do not rush past that sentence while looking for your pot of gold. Making your calls *is* the gold.

Okay, I put it out there. I feel better, and I hope you do, too. My guess is, however, you want something else; you want something more. As the quote above describes, "the *obvious* really is almost impossible to see." Here are fourteen more chapters on *The DNA of Business: for Network Marketing.* I hope you enjoy reading it, learning from it and coming to realize the obvious— you can stop "working too hard, and thinking too much" by just *making your calls.*

# SECTION 1

# Dream and Belief

*"To accomplish great things, we must not only act but also **DREAM**, not only plan but also **BELIEVE**."*

- Anatole France

## CHAPTER ONE

# DREAM: I Googled It

*"You have to Dream, to have a Dream to come true."*

- Eric Golden

*(I know I am not the first person to say this; but, I Googled it and couldn't find a credited author—not even that guy 'Anonymous'. So, I am taking it! If I'm not known for anything else, at least I will be known for that.)*

Y OU HAVE TO HAVE a DREAM to have a Dream come true is a silly statement. Thinking you can invest a few bucks on a book that teaches you how to build a business when you did not bring your Dream with you is nonsensical. Even crazier is how you will read every page, memorize every technique, and think you're ready to sponsor the world, and you will still leave your strongest player in the locker room. The Dream, or a lack thereof, is the single most reliable forecast for your success (or failure).

The Dream, being the first element in the DNA-*b* model, is the starting point on your journey to success. As you come to accept this, you will further understand how Belief (the second element) only becomes relevant after your Dream is solidified. Your Dream has to be alive. Investing the time and work necessary at the beginning, with the end in mind, is crucial. Why are you building this business? What do you want out of it? What do you want out of life? DNA-*b* will provide you details to obtaining your Dream, but you must have one in the first place.

The breakdown of the DNA-*b* model was deciphered in the introduction—the DREAM and BELIEF elements are the base-pair foundation for the RESULTS you seek. They act as *active* and *passive* agencies, playing off each other, with the Dream asking permission to move ahead and the Belief giving it permission. This base pair is a couplet, and although they are developed individually, understanding that they are dancing partners—like yin and yang or sweet and sour—is important. The Dream is the *positive* component of the pairing while Belief is the *negative*. Too much of one overpowers the other, sending success reeling into a black hole. Suffice it to say, if the key to success in real estate is "location, location, location," and in acting it is "practice, practice, practice," you will soon recognize true business Results comes from "Dream and Belief, Dream and Belief, Dream and Belief."

Just as a Dream has layers in a sleep cycle, likewise, when we discuss the Dream element, Dreams in life have levels. In network marketing (NM), Dreaming at all financial levels has purpose. You will come to appreciate how a small win early in your career leads to huge wins later on. When you succeed in obtaining your smaller Dreams, you will gain confidence to Dream bigger. Regardless of the size of your Dream, a

## DNA-*b*

> "The Dream's direct byproduct, motivation, is an amazing ally."

measly $100 to comfortably go out to dinner, or a million-dollar home with a helipad, you will learn the motivation (*positive*) comes from the same place, feels the same way, and needs to be nurtured in the same manner.

In 1987, I truly came to understand the relevance of a Dream. I was sitting at one of my first NM conventions, where thousands of people gathered to hear stories and techniques from our company's leadership. The featured speaker was Dex-

DNA-*b*

ter Yager, quite possibly the most successful network marketer in history. I will never forget one of the things he said, *"If the Dream is big enough, the facts don't count."* This was the first time I had heard this phrase, and since then, I have pondered its meaning numerous times. I not only thought about it, but I probably repeated it a thousand times. "If the Dream is big enough, the facts don't count," has proven accurate in my life. But, I sure needed some help with the "facts" many times.

Some twenty-five years detached from my early "Dexter Yager" moment, I now understand not only the power of the Dream, but also its requirement to be at the beginning of all things accomplished. The Dream is what gets you off the couch to show the plan after a long day at work. It is what motivates you to stop in the middle of a hectic day to make those follow-up phone calls with a prospect from the night before. It is the only thing propelling you to kiss your kids good-bye after din-ner, knowing the short time away from them today will soon be replaced with a lifetime of family memories. You do these things because your Dreams have positioned themselves to be relevant to your life. It is that look in your eye saying, "I am on a mission, and everybody is getting in!" And, at the end of the day when your head hits the pillow, you drift away again to recharge yourself for another chance to make your Dreams come true.

Realizing Dreams can be both *tangible* (things purchased with money) and *intangible* (things you benefit from over time) is paramount. A Dream can be *positive* (things you're running toward) or *negative* (things you're running from). If the purpose of a Dream is to create motivation, then anything that causes you to react will do. Simply put, whether it is a new car, time with your family, enough money in the bank, or a way out of a job, if you want it bad enough to do something to get it—it's a Dream!

Dreams come in as many shapes and sizes as the Dreamer. As I've traveled over the years from America to Asia, no matter who I meet, white collar to blue collar, or young women to elderly men, the Dreams we all hold are centered on three basic concepts: We all want what is best for our *families*, our *futures*, and *ourselves*. Our various genetics, upbringings, and experiences cause us to Dream for different tangible things. The intangible things are quite often similar and are normally at the root of our motivation. Every human being has an inner desire for freedom and control, and this is the driving force that says, "I can do it. I am worthy. I will succeed!"

> ### DNA-*b*
>
> **"If time and money were no problem, what would you do with your life?"**

Develop a "ladder of Dreams," comprised of many Dreams at many different price points. Each rung on the ladder allows you to *receive* while you *achieve*. Along the way, you will also gain Belief while you acquire your Dreams. This will be critical, because the interplay with Belief will only allow you to act on Dreams suitably paired. Your Dream ladder may include: $100 for a date night, $300 on something for the kids, $500 a month for a new car, $800 a month to support your parents, or $1,000 a month to help pay the mortgage—these tangibles drive you to perform. If you want a lifestyle of spending four-figures on season tickets, five-figures on a nice vacation, and six-figures on a yacht or new home, the thrill of the chase is worth the effort. The tangible Dream is the easiest to identify and, most often, the initial motivator.

*Author comment: Literary guidelines dictate I use "he" and "him" to represent a single individual. This, in no way, is intended to offend any "she" or "her."*

Nothing makes someone *want* more than the feeling he gets when he sees the perfect car or beautiful estate home. I am told some women get the same feeling when they see a pair of shoes. I will have to take their word for it. What is it about the tangible things that make us all giddy?

In addition to the things that make us *look* good, some things truly make us *feel* good. This is where the intangible lives. The intangible can be identified in two categories: the things that allow us to enjoy our time, and the pride we feel in the accomplishments along the way. I know driving down the road in a Ferrari can make us feel good, but purchasing a roomful of computers for our child's school is truly touching.

You will always enjoy the tangible, but harnessing the power of the intangible Dream comes from deep within your soul. The biggest, the brightest, and the fastest things will still have their appeal, but the freedoms of time and security with the ones you love have special significance. Intangible things make us feel like we are sitting on the top of the world!

Travel Dreams combine both the tangible and the intangible. Vacations give us time away from the pressures of life, phones, bosses, employees, and conflict and are a perfect way to connect with what is possible. They provide an opportunity to recharge our batteries while climbing our Dream ladder to financial freedom. Plan some pleasure trips along the way as rewards for fiscal or rank accomplishments and money becomes more abundant.

You now have a perspective on tangible and intangible Dreams. Here is more on what makes a Dream positive or negative. Some Dreams are things we are running towards: a nicer car, more money in the bank, a trip to Italy, or spending time with our family. These are what I call positive Dreams. Examples of negative Dreams are a failing car, a job you hate, and overdue bills. Nagging problems can be as much, or even more, of a motivator than positive Dreams. You can focus on the problem or focus on the solution, whichever motivates you the most.

> ### DNA-*b*
>
> "All our Dreams can come true, if we have the courage to pursue them."
> – Walt Disney

When asked the proverbial networking question, "What would you do with your life if time and money were no issue?" your mind comes alive and unlimited possibilities creep onto your Dream board. You need to know this industry creates residual incomes large enough to make all of it possible.

Dreaming and coming up with reasons to build your Business is child's play compared to the maturity required to maintain your vision, especially in the face of adversity. Ensuring your Dreams can sustain the length of your journey will take work. Where a new car and a bank account can be quickly identified off the top of your head, the maintenance of your Dream life will take time and effort.

Dreams are interesting. Consider with me the Dream Wheel concept. As a child, we had no problem Dreaming of things we wanted. Children say things like, "When I grow up, I want to be an astronaut and go on a rock-

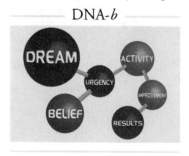

DNA-*b*

et ship." Or, "When I grow up, I want a horse," and "When I grow up, I want to be a doctor, a firefighter, or a policeman." Do you remember saying, "When I grow up, I want to have a million dollars and live in a big house?" Dreaming as a child is easier because at that age, we think anything is possible.

Then, we get older, and the reality of life seems to get in the way. We learn everything has a price to pay, and we may not have enough to get in. What happens then? Our Dream Wheel slows, eventually stops, and then rusts in place. Then, we are struck by *lightning*, smack-dab in the middle of our head. How does this happen? A friend takes us out to lunch, draws circles on a yellow pad, and before we know it, the wheel rotates. We joined network marketing, and we're reading a book about DNA.

## CHAPTER TWO

# DREAM: Do You Have a Refrigerator?

*"I Dream for a living."*

- Steven Spielberg

I F YOU ARE STILL reading at this point, you now have a concept of a Dream. So let's take advantage of your spinning Dream wheel and keep it moving. In fact, let's talk about things you can do to make it go faster and ensure it never slows down again! The two keys to Dream maintenance are: 1) Continually adding to your Dream list, and 2) Never losing sight of what you are working toward—I mean this literally—*never* losing sight.

Adding to your Dream list can be easy if you are aware of everything around you. Many Dreams are visible. They are things you can see as you go about your daily life—in magazines, on television, at a shopping center, and even driving down the road. Wherever you happen to look, Dreams are everywhere. Be open to what is possible. The more you interact with the outside world, the more you can take whatever you like for your own purpose. Hey, it's a Dream!

I have also found Dreams by hanging around other Dreamers. I like to be with people who not only want more out of life, but they also do the things necessary to get it. They live life to the fullest, and often have the lifestyle to prove it. Wanting "things" from their lifestyle isn't wrong, as long as you do what is right to acquire them. Even daydreamers, who never intend on doing anything about their lot in life, can be a conduit for your vision. Always be sure you have a true emotional connection to what you are after. A Rolex® may look good on someone else but might not stand the test of time motivating you.

While you can connect with the desire from the tangible Dream in an instant, the intangibles are driven by the human spirit and often take time to sew themselves into your soul. They make your eyes tear, your throat close, and your chest swell. They are the really good things in life. Owning a castle or flying a jet is really cool, but, you'll never replace the feeling of sponsoring someone's kid through college or happily taking care of your parents as they age. Gosh, I really do love this stuff!

> ### DNA-*b*
>
> "If you want more than you have now, Dream more than you do now."

Through association and awareness, put yourself in a position to add things you long for to your list. You will periodically need to draw strength from this list as you move through the DNA-*b* model. You have to Dream Big—*big enough so the facts don't count.*

Years ago, I gave a speech entitled, "Realistic Dreams . . . Realistic Commitments." It received a lot of play through the NM world. (This audio link may be found at: www.TheDNAofBusiness.com.) The gist is the importance of first owning a realistic Dream before you are able to make a realistic commitment.

We must also grasp what realistic means in relation to our Dream. What is realistic to one person may be far-fetched to another. My definition, therefore, is "A realistic Dream is a Dream, desire, or goal that has flowed through this process: I

DNA-*b*

see it, I want it, I really want it, and I think—what would I have to do to get it?" The Dream does not ever entertain the possibility of failure. In fact, the minute your mind asks the question, "What would I have to do to get it?" your mind shifts to *answering*—the Dream part ends, and the commitment part begins. The Dream has no limits; it's a Dream.

The far-fetched Dream is one where your mind's progression goes like this: You see it, you want it, you really want it, and you think— you could never have it. If you never entertain the "What do I have to do to get it?"—it isn't a realistic Dream. Although you can Dream about anything, the *realistic* Dream is one you *think* you can possibly have—before you consider actually *believing* it. When an unbelievable Dream comes to mind, it is not a Dream the DNA-*b* can deliver. Although, the Dream is dependent on Belief, if you cannot separate the two, it becomes too difficult to achieve.

Without restraints, we can easily add to our lists on a regular basis. Both realistic and far-fetched Dreams qualify. Just write down the realistic Dream you believe now, and the far-fetched for your Dream life, which may become realistic as your Belief increases. They both work. Remember, a Dream is what motivates you to get out and make the phone calls, drive the miles, and continue to work on yourself along the way. The Dreams you have must be real, they must be big enough, and they must be *yours*.

For most people, the problem is not being able to identify the things they want. The challenge is to maintain the motivation as your focus shifts toward doing the work. Dream maintenance has as much to do with keeping your eye on the prize as it does with keeping your eyes open to new things. By accomplishing the smaller ones, you reinforce not only the model you are following, but also strengthen your Belief you have become more than you used to be. With every success comes a new confidence, a renewed you—a certainty motivates you to strive for more. A conviction pushes you to strive for levels you originally thought impossible. What becomes possible becomes probable; what becomes probable becomes likely; what becomes likely becomes reality!

### DNA-*b*

> "The minute you claim a Dream for yourself, this is when success begins."

For a boy who Dreams of catching the winning pass as time runs out in the Super Bowl, he must first find motivation for playing hard in his pee-wee league. If he is fortunate enough to do well at an early age, his Belief that he can make it strengthens. This method of small wins leading to a bigger victory never changes. Listen to an interview by this same boy (Michael Strahan, Super Bowl XLII Champion), now an NFL player readying for his championship game, "We just took it one game at a time."

Another famous NM phrase by Earl Nightingale is, "Success

is the progressive realization of a worthwhile Dream or goal." This means you actually start to succeed the moment you take your first step. Your goal might be total financial freedom, but most people aren't strong enough to make the marathon run— not without help. Staying the course requires the periodic drink and people along the road clapping, cheering, and encouraging you on toward the finish line.

During the *progressive realization,* how do you keep your Dream in sight and never lose touch with it? The technique I have used, taught, and believe in, will only take a few minutes to explain. It is a take-off of your usual practices, and you probably never realized its effect.

Consider this: Why do you place pictures of your family and friends in your wallet and at work? Why do you put photos, report cards, and notes on your refrigerator at home? They are constant reminders of things we don't want to forget—people and priorities.

Do you have a refrigerator? For as long as I have been in NM, I have owned a side-by-side refrigerator. Just so you know, I am confident this will also work with an upper-lower unit, too. I cut out pictures of all the things I wanted (tangible and intangible) and placed them on my fridge, necessitating a whole bunch of mini-magnets to do it just right. If you are interested in posting pictures on your refrigerator, include everything you can think of—from the smallest of your Dreams through the things you presently think are almost impossible. I had everything from a scoop of ice cream to yachts and international travel brochures.

When I began using this method for Dreaming, I had young children. Pictures of ice cream cones were rewards they could grasp for when I was away during some evenings. This also helped me, because time with my children was on my Dream ladder. With a picture of a double-scooped sugar cone of sweet, dripping ice cream, the Golden family was learning a life-changing lesson. My children learned patience and sacrifice paid off, and I demonstrated how focused Activity provides predictable Results.

We eventually had hundreds of pictures spend time on the refrigerator door. They "passed across" because the freezer door was their final destination. Every time the Dream was achieved, I moved the corresponding picture to the freezer. This is one of the magical aspects of this method. Physically moving the picture from one side to the other, we are able to feel the ac-complishment. Every time we pass by or open the doors, we are able to gain motivation from the things on the fridge *and* con-fidence from the pictures on the freezer. This may sound a bit elementary, but it works—and it will work for you!

To accentuate the effective-ness of picture motivation, af-fix a photo of your face within a cut-out picture of your Dream. Put yourself in the Mercedes convertible, on a chaise lounge

> ### DNA-*b*
>
> "Dreams may have different price tags and lev-els of satisfaction, but they all burn as kindling in the fire that fuels your soul."
> -Me (Eric Golden)

on the beach in Fiji, with your family in the center of Yosemite, and maybe helping other people meet their needs. These things make life worth living, so Dream it up, and then work to *live* it up. Countless articles have been written about the importance of visualization, so use it to your advantage.

Initially placing my first set of Dream pictures was excit-ing, but the day I noticed more than a hundred items had been moved over to the freezer side was beyond gratifying! Imagine how you will feel when this happens for you—and it will!

## CHAPTER THREE

# BELIEF: Fear Based . . . Dream Driven

*"Fear based . . . Dream driven."*

- Eric Golden

H OW WOULD YOU FEEL if I said your Beliefs are not real? I am not saying they are not; I am only asking the question. The same emotion that causes you to disagree with me strongly causes most people to fail in NM and many other things in life as well. Oh, Belief—if only we could get a handle on your power over us.

The second element in the DNA-*b* is *Belief.* If the Dream is the *motivator*, then the Belief is *the limiter.* When the Dream says, "jump," the Belief says, "not so high." Belief generally has no factual reason for its limiting tendencies other than fear of getting hurt. Make no mistake, you have plenty of historical reasons why Belief wants to protect you, but until you realize how to deal with your fear, you will never be able to move ahead.

If we research the word Belief in the dictionary, we will find the top five definitions include these descriptive words: *emotion, confidence, accepts, opinion,* and *faith*.[4] These are all subjective. This means we are choosing what to believe. These words imply we should have control over our Belief; on the contrary, our Belief has control over us. Fear is where Belief evolves. Regardless if our fear is founded or unfounded, it affects our every move. Your Belief is limited because your fear obliterates all confidence or faith. Fear is what your Belief must defeat; it must be calmed, ignored, or eliminated.

In relation to Belief, you must take steps to calm, eliminate, or ignore your fear. Belief is a summation of the information you have on an issue, coupled with the way you feel about it. If you access more information, you may be in a position to change your level of Belief. I know the Dream is big enough and, therefore, the facts shouldn't count. But, Belief, according to *Merriam-Webster*, isn't purely the facts. The Dream can trump the facts, but Belief is a whole different animal. My job at this point is to convince you how your Belief (and its level of emotion) can change over time. You just have to know how to do it.

> ## DNA-*b*
>
> "Feelings are not a byproduct of your Belief, they are its creator."
>
> -Me, again

I submit the following: Dreams are real. In most cases, you can touch a car, a bank account, and hug your children at the park on a Thursday afternoon. You can hit the snooze button on your alarm clock as often as you want or never set it at all. Why not give money or time to your parents or charity, buy season tickets to see your favorite football team or this year's opera series, and walk through the mall with enough money in your pocket to do serious damage? You touch it; you feel it. You got it? These are DREAMS! Even the intangible Dream is touched by your soul. You know what they are, and they truly motivate you. You know why you like them. The key to knowing it is a Dream is if you really don't care whether anyone else agrees. It's *your* Dream!

DNA-*b*

Beliefs, on the other hand, only *feel* real. Unlike the object of your Dreams, you already possess your Belief. They are most often things you cannot touch, but they touch you.

You often cannot tell why you believe them—other than saying, "Because I do," and you always care whether others agree. Other people's opinions are often the primary reason you believe one way or another in the first place.

Do you believe what you do because you are told what to believe, or is it because you feel it? If you *feel* it, then why? These questions are never ending, and volumes have been written about Belief by psychology professors from every university.

Whether you are new to NM or have been around the industry for a while, you bring a certain set of experiences commonly affecting your Belief in succeeding. The first thing to go must be any Beliefs that do not support your new aspirations or Dreams. These Beliefs, although foundationally supported from your life's experiences, are subject to change. Changing your Beliefs will require acceptance that change is not only possible, but desired. Desiring change is a necessity. These *change* factors include new information and evidence directly conflicting with your old Beliefs. In fact, after exercising a change in your

Beliefs, you will discover you can change the way you feel about many things, often easier than you ever thought possible. This is simply a learned process. You want your Belief to change—you gather information and evidence . . . you gain a new perspective . . . you change your Belief.

Beliefs can be an obstacle to your success and are almost always seeded in a garden of some sort of fear. I choose not to use the ever-popular explanation, *False Evidence Appearing Real* to prove my "Belief is not real" theory. This never really helped me get over my fear, so I won't push it on you, either. Being afraid of heights comes from a fear of falling. Being afraid of snakes comes from fear of being bitten. Being afraid of tight spaces comes from a fear of running out of air. In each of these cases, the Belief is only real because of a fear. You could know (Belief) the tall building won't fall, the snake is dead, and a tube will pump air constantly, but you might still be afraid. Belief, especially negative Belief, has something to do with logic and is controlled by emotional *fear*.

> ### DNA-*b*
>
> "What the mind of man can conceive and Believe, it can achieve."
> -Napoleon Hill

New information, however, does have a tremendous affect on your Belief. Would your Belief be fortified if someone on the building's rooftop were holding you firmly? What if the snake lay unmoving for an hour? In the case of the DNA-*b*, we will be dealing with things far less critical, although they may feel similar, than the snake thing giving us the heebie-jeebies. Being fearful of what your friends may think, wasting a little time, or possibly failing yet again are fears, which in turn, create networking Belief issues. Do these really compare? Oddly enough, I say they do! Being frozen in place because of a snake on your path is no different than a fear keeping you from making a call. They both keep you from what you want. The good news is this fear/Belief relationship can all be transformed from one that controls you to one that will empower you.

For the time being, suspend your thoughts regarding your ability to succeed in building a network. Go off the grid into a completely different time and place. I want to show you the processes that guide your mind into believing one way or another. This Belief directly affects your behavior. Realizing these processes exist will provide you with the ability to do something about them. Interrupt the process, and change the Belief.

Imagine yourself at ten-years old in an elementary school auditorium. I am presenting a slide show of photos of my trip around the world. The screen is filled with breathtaking shots of the Eiffel Tower, the Alps, St. Peter's Basilica, children playing soccer on the beaches in Brazil, sailfish jumping in the waves of the Caribbean, wild animals roaming the African plain, and each slide more beautiful than the one before. At ten, your mind goes through this process: travel around the world—that would be cool; see all those things—that would be fun. Not having to attend school—I want to go! The initial thoughts coming to your mind are all POSITIVE. Then, even as a child, the NEGATIVE thoughts creep in. I am afraid to fly; I may not like the food; and my parents will never take me anyway. If this strikes a chord, then I submit, as adults, we go through the exact same mindset of the *positive*-to-*negative* process.

Watching this same lecture today, I am confident the same cool, fun, and vacation thoughts would run through your mind. As adults, however, the negative comes even quicker. We start thinking, "I can't get time away; I don't have the money," and "I need to do other things first."

This start positive and end negative thought process causes Belief to be an inhibiting force in our lives. The world traveler story exemplifies how we develop a pattern of thinking at an early age, and adjust it as we grow older. Once you recognize this, changing these patterns can diffuse the negative emotions, while reinforcing the positive ones. This ultimately shifts your Belief, unlocks the limits restricting you, and enables you to move ahead more aggressively—believing you will succeed. Again, I submit—interrupt the process and change the Belief.

An automobile's gas gauge is a great representation of the re-

DNA-*b*

lationship between your Dream and Belief. The "F" indicates a full tank or a full Dream, and the "E" represents an empty Belief or an impossible Dream. In this example, your Belief ranges from negative to neutral (or like half a tank), and you know when your tank is half full that you will need something more to complete the journey. The Dream takes you from a neutral mid-point to the positive outcome you seek. As discussed in Chapter One, the Dream can come from negative situations, but it is still a positive motivator. Similarly, Belief can also be positive or negative, but fear, which is at the center of Belief, is negative in our model. At best, Belief can only bring you to the point where the Dream can take control. The best Belief can deliver is the freedom to act, but it doesn't propel you to action.

Want a better word picture? Think of the top half of the gauge being the Dream, and the bottom half representing your Belief level. When your tank is full, you can drive for hours without any expected concern, and you remain excited about where you are going. When you see the gauge dipping down toward empty, you have a very different experience. Depending on how quickly you can get gas and how much money you have, fear may set in. You fixate on how much gas costs, whether you'll find a station in time, and whether stopping fits into your schedule. Your mind becomes consumed with the problematic things happening in your life. When money is tight or you are on a stretch of road where you can't find a gas station, your Dream is replaced by a lack of Belief, or fear, and you are reduced to survival mode.

A different type of representation could be made to clarify the Dream/Belief relationship. When you believe you live in a great country, it allows you to take a stance emotionally. It doesn't necessarily cause you to argue or go to war. The Dream is your desire to convince someone your country is great. Your motivation to engage someone else in defending your Belief is the Dream's role. The Dream is doing the work when you are willing to speak out or act out, even when you are only defending your position against someone who confronts you. Because of Belief, you are willing to risk the pending success or failure. It has processed the possible outcomes and has silently spoken. Belief readies you for battle—the Dream fights the war.

Too often, people find themselves stuck in neutral, caught in a place where a clean handoff between the two elements is missing. Most often this occurs because you don't understand the need for Belief's acceptance of the possible before Dream's motivation to achieve. A deep-seeded Dream can reach across the neutral line and drag Belief some of the way for a short period of time, but this is never long-lasting. If you are strong in Belief but still find yourself in neutral, you need a bigger Dream to move on.

## CHAPTER FOUR

# BELIEF: Three Questions

*"The constant assertion of Belief is an indication of fear."*

- Jiddu Krishnamurti

THE DNA-*b* BELIEF ELEMENT is developed by using it. Just like a muscle, you strengthen it by exercise. If you never establish Belief, then it will never come to your rescue when you are challenged.

You will look for the answers to three questions when asked to join a NM company. Joining a company has more to do with how a business looks. Building a business, on the other hand, has more to do with *how* it feels, and we will cover this in the next chapter.

These first three questions are purely based on what brought you to the presentation the day you saw it: your experiences, what is going on in your life at that moment, and whether you are looking for something to change. If the stars align, you sign up.

Deciding to join a NM business is often done quickly. Deciding to actually build one, for some, can take forever. The reason most people take a significant amount of time is the need to exercise their core Beliefs and fully develop that muscle.

Let's play this out: You are sitting in a friend's living room watching a person you have never seen before draw circles on a whiteboard (oops, I just dated myself). How about this: You are sitting in a friend's living room watching a video of someone drawing circles. At some point during the presentation, three questions come to your mind. They dwell in your subconscious without ever interrupting your focus, and at sometime before the night is through, their answers will direct your decision.

- Can I do it?

- Is it worth it?

- Where will I find the time?

These are the Belief questions that must be answered before you will allow yourself to sign up in NM. These questions involve the Dream, but they go deeper than that. What is amazing is most people will process these almost instantaneously, always subconsciously, and then make a quick decision whether or not to move ahead. I am sure you have been to a meeting where the presenter asked you to go ahead and get started tonight. The effectiveness of this closing remark has to do with the predetermined answers you don't realize you have already made. Your decision is based on whether

> ### DNA-*b*
>
> "The process of making a decision is more important than the length it takes to make it."

you have been provided the right information for you to agree that *you can do it, you want it, and you have (or will make) the time.*

Although you have answered these questions before you signed up, at various times throughout your building career, you will revisit them. When this happens, your new answers may be different, because you will have accumulated more experiences, something else inevitably is happening in your life, and you may (or may not) be looking to change something. Since these questions are so important to your outcome, let me provide some of the reasoning that should keep your Belief tank full.

## Can I Do It?

This one is simple to answer. Look at the contact list on your phone and the database for your e-mail. Ask yourself if any of the people listed may be interested in your product. Then ask if any of these people may want (or need) to earn more money.

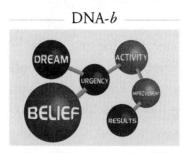

DNA-*b*

Remember, some people may want or need more money, even if you don't know about them. This is where we complicate things but don't have to. We begin to wonder, "What am I going to say to them? What are they going to think of me?" This is normal, and we will help you handle these concerns or fears. For now, answer this: If you did ask each person on your contact list one question, "Will you look at something?" do you believe some of them would say, "Yes?" Hey, you can do it. Don't fight me on this. Not everyone is going to look—and you know it. The reason you make this harder on yourself is you fail to remember you can't get everyone to do anything, but you can often get some people to do something. Why should this be any different?

## Is it Worth it?

This one isn't much harder. Picture your refrigerator door completely covered with the Dreams you want in your life. Now look at the freezer side. Do you see all the empty space? This is where your Dreams become reality—on the freezer side! If you really want to know if it is worth it, ask yourself this: "If I don't build this business, how many of these Dreams will I probably get?" If you still need reinforcement, start taking the things off the refrigerator you are willing to let go. You will quickly see more money and time are needed for the things you want—or you can't have them. So, is it worth it?

## Where Will I Find the Time?

Okay, this one will take some effort. I am well aware you are already working overtime, your mother is sick, next week is the church revival where you have bounce house responsibility, your kids need to get to soccer practice, and that man of yours is never around when you need him. You have no time! Well, you may not like this answer, but you have to settle it for yourself once and for all.

Look at your refrigerator Dream board. Then look at the contact list in your phone. You already think it is worth it, and you can do it. Am I right? So how are you going to handle the time question? For the truly busy person, everything is about priorities. For most others, though, they could manage their time more wisely. No matter your circumstance, I will provide you a proven strategy to start your business with as little as five minutes a day—if you can make a five-minute commitment. My "5-Minute Bank Account" program (chapters 10, 11, and 12) can create a base of business, allowing you to compound your time by leveraging other people's efforts into more productive hours than you could ever work on your own.

I admit building a business with time restrictions is not only difficult, it is not much fun either. You know you can do it, but you have to make your prize *worth it*. Only then will you find or make the time.

Throughout my decades in the NM industry, I have heard almost every reason for why people can't do the business. Don't be fooled! Usually, it has to nothing to do with their specific question or comment. Although the objections they provide seem real to them, the real reason is a lack of "yes" answers to the three Belief questions, and they don't even realize it.

> DNA-*b*
>
> "Whether you think you can or you think you can't, you're right."
> -Henry Ford

Trainers often teach you to use the Dream when answering objections. Dreaming with them is *very effective if the Dream is big enough*, but remember the Dream alone only directly answers the, "Is it worth it?" question.

Most often, your prospect believes the issue is being able to do it or finding the time. This is the true hurdle—learning how to interpret their question. When you respond accordingly, you will greatly Improve your sponsoring rate. The best way to handle any objection is to prevent it from being raised. The best way to prevent objections from arising is to address them in your presentation. By clearly conveying information to your prospect that answers their Belief questions, you have a much better chance of a successful meeting. If objections do come up, be sure to answer the direct question and then steer the conversation back to processing the answers you are seeking.

CAUTION! Your job is not to get them to join your business. Your job is to help them answer the question in an honest fashion, giving them the right information so they will answer "yes" if they want more and are willing to do more to get it.

As I said, most people make a decision to join a NM company fairly quickly because on the surface, the upside potential, getting what they want, is worth the downside risk, normally a few hundred bucks. Although they are prepared to do a little work and expect to experience small financial rewards in return, they often fail to think through the length of time required to make most of their Dreams come true.

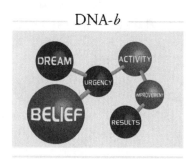

DNA-*b*

"Just take a season of your life," is the common rallying cry from NM leadership. These leaders often fail to mention, though, that a season in NM is normally two to five years. I'm quite sure most people have trouble seeing past the next few months, much less the next two to five years. Therefore, I'm not sure anyone can truly make an initial commitment to a season longer than a winter, spring, summer, or fall.

Nevertheless, as you get entrenched in the NM culture, you gain appreciation for the process as you see yourself and others succeed. This raises Belief and allows your Dream to motivate you further. You will only commit to the length of time that is consistent with your Belief. You can come in with a little Belief and succeed. This can carry you through the initial period of building, while strengthening itself for a longer run. A million-dollar lifestyle is available to you, but fortifying your Belief is crucial to earning the money needed to really change your life.

Before I explain how to sustain yourself through the process, I must caution you to beware of the *Dream stealer*. The Dream stealer is someone who robs you of the vision for a better and more enjoyable life. This thief comes in two forms—people you know, and others, who, believe it or not, you will never meet. Rather than address why you may let others steal your Dream, I will share the motivation of those who do the stealing.

People are people. I never really understood the meaning of this until I started my NM career. Most are nice, but *all* are quirky. Say "Hello" to the wrong person on the wrong day, and whammo!" It happens, right? Your Belief will often be tested when you talk with people you know or people you meet. The people you know are particularly dangerous because of the relationships you share.

We often feel obligated to accept what people say to us, without regard to why they are commenting or reacting in a certain way. These people will also subconsciously process the Belief questions before they respond to you. If they have not seen what you have seen, then they cannot feel what you feel. Let me clarify this: they don't have the same information, and so they will unlikely have the same perspective. Make sense?

Everyone speaks from a position of his own Belief. Friends and family who love you try to protect you from those things they fear:

> *A spouse*—A spouse can become emotional when he or she believes you are going to spend more time and money away from home.
>
> *Friends*—They have seen you start other things, and they

have little confidence you will see this one through to the end.

*Co-workers*—They accept you for whom you are, and now they do not want you to change.

*People you respect*—They feel responsible for you, and they do not want their opinion to send you on a journey Resulting in you getting hurt.

The Dream stealers you will never meet are found on the Internet. This is dangerous for you, because you have no point of reference to their experiences. They have one goal: to keep you from getting involved, and without knowing anything about them, you should not give their information any credence. I know this sounds like a "I knew that's what Eric would say" answer, but, come on now, what did you expect? Who are these people, anyway?

In many cases, the Dream stealer's goal is to create doubt in your company, so he can cross recruit you into his. If you want to spend time on the web, go to your company's website, rather than engage in a generic search of people who have any number of reasons to stop you. You may think your NM company has a slanted opinion of itself. On the other hand, why would you ever take advice from somebody on the web who signs his opinion, "Bob A, from Jacksonville?"

Your goal is to succeed in creating the life and lifestyle you desire. To accomplish this, do not re-evaluate your Belief. Protecting yourself from controllable setbacks should be a priority. The people you know want you to be happy and are not trying to hurt you. They just don't know what you know. The people you *don't* know don't really care about you or your happiness. In both cases, you need to rely on *your* answers to the three Belief questions.

Ultimately, you have control over the words defining Belief. Your emotion and confidence determine what you accept; your opinion and faith ultimately determine your Belief.

## CHAPTER FIVE

# BELIEF: Are You Hard Core?

Luke Skywalker: *"I can't believe it."*

Yoda: *"That is why you fail."*

- Characters from George Lucas, Star Wars Movies

**A**RE YOU IN GREAT health right now? If you aren't, can you remember a time when you were a better version of yourself health wise? When you have good health, with no nagging pains or problems, you rarely even think about health issues. If your back is sore, your eyes begin to fail, or you have weight issues causing you to feel out of shape, then your health constantly occupies your mind. It affects everything you do. Similarly, you don't tend to question your level of Belief along your journey to business success, unless something negative (a fear) introduces itself. It can be something someone says or something you read, but it throws you into discomfort, causing you to doubt your answers to the questions: "Can I do it?" "Is it worth it?" and "Do I have the time?"

Anything causing you to question your Belief in what you are doing is as unhealthy to your business as a physical ailment is to your body. Knowing what to do when this happens can mean life or death for your financial future.

We have discussed how to develop your Dream and how to use pictures to maintain your vision. You now understand Belief also needs to be strengthened. This is the only way you will have control over adjusting, ignoring, or eliminating the fears that cause you to doubt. Your responses to the three qualifying Belief questions have allowed you to join a business, and so the time has come to get to work. How nice that would be if that were the case. As the saying goes, "If it were that easy, everyone would do it."

Your Dream is alive; what could possibly get in your way? The most common reason someone with a Dream remains stuck in neutral is a problem with their *Core Beliefs*. We have eight Core Beliefs, and each one needs to be healthy in order for us to move ahead.

# DNA-*b*

### Eight Core Beliefs

| Hard Core | Soft Core |
|---|---|
| 1. Belief in the Industry | 5. Belief in the System |
| 2. Belief in the Company | 6. Belief in your Upline |
| 3. Belief in the Product | 7. Belief in your Sponsor |
| 4. Belief in the Comp Plan | 8. Belief in Yourself |

Most people have high levels of Belief in some of their Core Beliefs when they first start. Not fortifying the other Beliefs, where they are lacking, will cause hesitation. Not fortifying the other Beliefs will cause hesitation. A weakness in any one of them can be degrading as well. As we learned in the last few chapters, Belief is subjective. When one Belief begins to be questioned, your perspective shifts, and you look differently at the other Core Beliefs—thus, the "one bad apple spoils the whole bunch" analogy.

In this chapter, we will discuss the first four Core Beliefs: Industry, Company, Product, and Compensation— Hard Core Beliefs. They are hard variables because once you garner a Belief about them, your Belief should remain steady, without abrupt day-to-day changes. New in-formation and experiences may influence you a small amount, but your impression or Belief of the industry, company, product, and compensation has less to

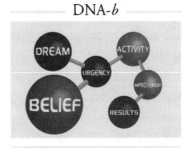

DNA-*b*

do with who you are than it does with what has been created for business purposes. If, as a whole, you are not confident in the industry, company, product, and compensation for the long run, your lack of Belief will inhibit your ability to start aggres-sively or end successfully.

The other four Core Beliefs (System, Upline, Sponsor, and Self) are considered Soft Core Beliefs. We will discuss them in the next chapter, but let me quickly say they are soft because they *do* conform to you. Your Belief will assuredly be influenced over time. Unlike Hard Core Beliefs, your constant interaction with the Soft Core variables will affect your day-to-day feelings in a big way.

The first step in developing any Core Belief is accumulating positive information. The second step involves gaining sufficient experience to imprint a positive, emotional pattern. Remember, according to *Merriam-Webster*, Belief is something based on emotion, opinion, and faith. Accepted information gives you confidence. Therefore, before you willingly move ahead, gathering the right information from the right sources is paramount.

**Belief in Your Industry:** Shall we start with what makes network marketing similar to most conventional businesses? Both conventional businesses and NM usually require some amount of start-up capital. Laws govern what you can and cannot do. You pay taxes and receive tax deductions. You generally have the ability to sell your business, will it to your children, or quit it altogether. You are paid based on your efforts of selling products or performing services. You can recruit, encourage, and train a sales force to sell for you, which you will then be paid even more. By the way, the majority of people you approach will tell you, "No," "No, thank you," or "No way." Sound familiar?

The principal differences between NM and conventional businesses are these: 1) More people are becoming millionaires in NM than any time in history—arguably, more than in any other industry in the world. 2) Over 3,000 NM companies are doing business in the United States, and they cumulatively have over 15 million distributors, and have total sales revenues of $28.5 billion in 2010.[5] Warren Buffet and Donald Trump own NM companies.[6] US Presidents and Fortune 500 executives have been NM distributors[7] Recent studies show as many as 85 percent of all women in America who make over $100,000 do so through direct sales, which includes NM.[8] *Rich Dad Poor Dad* author Robert Kiyosaki says that developing a NM business is one of the best investments a person can make.[9] 3) *USA*

*Today* writes, "Social financial networking" is the place to be for those looking for opportunity in the next generation!"[10]

Need more? A great way to gather information about the network marketing industry is from the Direct Selling Association (DSA).[11] This is a one-hundred-year-old organization that accumulates and disseminates information for the general public to access. It has recorded information regarding most of the oldest, largest, and most successful companies operating in America. Other companies who haven't joined the DSA can also provide you a great business opportunity.

- More than four in five (82 percent) direct sellers have been with their current direct selling company for one year or more, and 34 percent for a minimum of five years.[12]

- Eighty-eight percent of direct sellers rate their personal experience in direct selling as excellent, very good, or good.[13]

- Eighty-five percent of direct sellers say direct selling meets or exceeds their expectations as a good way to supplement their income.[14]

Network marketing is almost the only vehicle in which anyone, from anywhere, no matter his or her education level, gender, or marital status, can invest as little as a few hundred dollars and turn it into an income far greater than most people make.

Although most people get involved in NM for the money, many will claim the social and personal development benefits in this industry are the hidden gem. Countless stories are told from people who joined a NM company for financial reasons and called the life-changing lessons they learned in the business worth their involvement—even if they didn't achieve their financial goals.

So why is NM under such scrutiny? I believe this stems from

people being harassed by friends and family to join them in business. This isn't the way it was supposed to be. The intention of the founders of the first NM organizations was to enlist people who wanted to represent and sell to people they knew who *wanted* to buy it. They introduced the concept of providing a financial incentive to recruit other distributors, if those individuals also wanted to be part of the effort. This would Result in more product sales and more people building a business and making money. Although these original intentions were quite honorable, the greed, need, and the desire to succeed have caused some distributors to become overzealous in the endeavor. A distributor's first goal should be to benefit his prospect in some way with the product. A prospect should only be recruited to build his or own business if open to the idea.

Asking people you know to do something you believe will benefit them isn't wrong. Even if your offer is heartfelt, this still can make the prospect feel pressured and uncomfortable, causing him or her to react oddly. This is not a bad thing;

> ### DNA-*b*
>
> "What do you want?
> When do you want it?
> What are you willing to
> do to get it?"

it is a different thing. Sometimes a relationship is already suited for a business type of interaction, and sometimes it is not. If you were a plumber, you would naturally do work for people you knew. But if you do not normally conduct business with friends, NM may definitely feel a little different to you both.

We all make some recommendations that are usual and customary. For instance, if you went to a movie, and it was a good movie, would you not recommend it? Remember, however, the minute you start trying to *sell* your product or opportunity to someone for your gain, rather than his or hers, you risk the relationship and perpetuate the NM image. NM is a great industry with an unfortunate stigma for some, so rise above it!

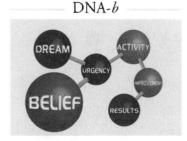

DNA-*b*

**Belief in Your Company:** A company's success truly begins with its ownership. Although the leaders in the field will ultimately be responsible for whether a company succeeds, these people will not engage properly if the company does not have the right ownership team. The decisions made from the top are vital to a company developing a solid foundation where success can germinate. In addition to good decision-making, the owner must possess adequate communication skills, strong financials, relevant business experience, and the ability to attract the proper people to the corporate management team.

To determine who's at the helm, you can gather corporate information from a number of sources. Company websites, corporate materials, and discussions with field leaders will provide you with all you need to know. When doing any type of research, be sure to consider sources credibility. All information, good and bad, will initially establish your Company Core Belief.

Information on company-promoted websites and corporate materials are often a good place to start. These are normally produced to show the company in the best light. With this said, the information found here usually is forthright, with many details that should provide you with a good general overview.

Your sponsor and upline will often provide you with solid information that has been passed down distributor-to-distributor.

"The owner has deep pockets," "The company's retention rate is phenomenal," and "The product is unbelievable" are standard recruiting phrases. This is not to say they aren't true, but, if you require knowing more, do your research.

The Internet offers a significant, but treacherous, research option. The general information on the web is the least reliable. The reason for this is simple. Although NM leadership created some credible websites, most people who are building a business successfully have very little time to post on the web; they are out creating their fortune. The people who blog, comment, start hate sites, and post videos on YouTube, are either people who weren't successful with a company, or are trying to recruit you to theirs. The problem here is you do not have any way to know what is real and what isn't. Some reputable groups have provided accurate information or written articles about a company, but unless the author is noteworthy, you should realize he probably has an agenda. In particular, be suspect of anyone whose name is "Anonymous."

> DNA-*b*
>
> "If you question anything, you have to question everything."
> – Ryan Chamberlin

**Belief in Your Product:** Are you ready for a strange comment, as if this is actually the first one in the book? Of the eight Core Beliefs, you will find your Product Core Belief is the least important of all—not because you don't need to believe in the product, but because you do. The reason this Belief is less significant is because you will gain Belief in the benefit when you use the product and will then own the Belief. No one will take it away from you. Belief is subjective and more information can change it, right? By trying the product, you will have all the data you require to Believe in it. If it works for you, you are good to go. Product Belief doesn't shift with what people say. Either you like it, or you don't. Either it makes your life better, or it doesn't. Testimonies can affect the way you feel, however, you will ultimately base your decision on your own experience.

Two other aspects need to be considered as you are developing Product Belief. Are you able to get excited discussing your product with prospects, and do you think your product has a market? This industry offers a myriad of items to sell, and you may find yourself considering something you, personally, wouldn't often use. This doesn't mean you can't get excited about the opportunity to represent it.

Being excited about something goes a long way when it is your second stream of income. The majority of people who join NM are looking for extra money. If possible, represent something you are passionate about. Selling a product you don't enjoy using can lead to a problem in your Product Belief. Knowing your item has a wide-open market is motivating. This alone can often feel more important than whether you use the product or enjoy talking about it. Be careful in this case, because as discussed in The Belief Element (chapter Three), a season in NM can take a while. Opportunity alone will not sustain your Product Core Belief.

**Belief in the Comp Plan:** Compensation is the monetary reward paid by a NM company to a distributor for selling the product. The company's compensation plan determines the method it calculates the payment. Belief in the comp plan comes from understanding enough about it to feel it is worthy of your time and effort. The amount of information needed by you or someone else to gain this Belief can vary dramatically, depending upon your personality, affinity for numbers, and trust. For some, knowing three sales pays you $100 is enough, while others want to know how many ways they can be paid, and how every bonus is calculated. Whatever your need, Comp Plan Core Belief can only be developed by asking the questions *you* need to ask.

The NM industry has a variety of compensation structures. They all have their benefits and drawbacks. Uni-level, matrix, binary, coded, and the newest hybrids can all be "spun" by a distributor when talking to a prospect. Telling you which type is best is impossible. The truth is, the best one for you is the one you believe you can make money from with the effort and ability you invest. It is an individual choice. If you sponsor a lot of people, you may notice a benefit to one Comp Plan versus another. If you retail products well, another plan might be more favorable. If you are good at team leadership, a third may compensate you for this skill. Even if one type is best for you, it may not be perfect for some of the people you recruit. See the dilemma?

> ### DNA-*b*
>
> "Do something you love, and you will never work a day in your life."
> — Confucius

Ultimately, a Belief in the compensation plan comes from a compilation of information we each need to know. For most, having a clear understanding of what type of organization and volume of sales is needed to break-even and create a bit of profitability is enough to feel and see a difference in the way we live.

## CHAPTER SIX

# BELIEF: Open Your Soft Core

Luke Skywalker: *"I am afraid."*

Yoda: *"Named must your fear be before banish it you can."*

- Characters from George Lucas, Star Wars Movies

THE SYSTEM IS THE framework of training methods and type of content that a company has in place for its distributors. A weak or underdeveloped System leads to a weak and underdeveloped field force. The System is responsible for both educating and motivating you.

**Belief in Your System:** Your sponsor and upline can enhance the System greatly, but these shouldn't be a requirement. If you bring a desire to succeed, willingness to learn, and work ethic, the System should be able to do the rest. Your Belief in the System is crucial to your utilizing its messages and in promoting it to your group. The possibility of your Business scaling to success beyond your own individual capacity is dependent on it.

The System makes vital and necessary information available to distributors. This content is designed to keep you informed of the most successful methods in building your business. The motivational aspect to a System's content, although sometimes denigrated by those outside of the NM industry, is the real key to its importance. When content is delivered to you in an inspirational manner, it increases your overall Belief in its effectiveness and your ability to use it. Whether it is a new contacting phrase, business presentation, or goal-setting method, the emotion it evokes in you is as important as the information itself. It should come across as fatherly advice wrapped in a mother's love. (Did I actually just write that? Trust me, if I could have thought of something better, I would have!)

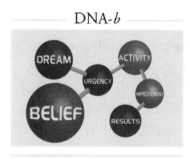

DNA-*b*

Network marketing is not only a legitimate business model, but its underlying principle of having independent agents operate a functional system is no different than what has made McDonald's Corporation the most world-renowned franchising opportunity on the PLANET. The McDonald's system spits out money through a duplicated, proven model.

Historically, company field leaders, who are distributors themselves, often developed a NM company's System. In recent years, more companies are providing Systems created by the company itself. In these circumstances, the corporate team usually includes former distributors, who have had successful field experiences. Companies who develop their own System, similarly, most likely communicate regularly with their current field leaders for suggestions and guidance.

When I started in NM, the System was simple. The information and motivation was delivered through cassette tapes (yes, I am that old!), books, and seminars. This provided me the knowledge and, along with *association* (time with others in my program), I gained Belief. Today, with advances in technology, the System's content can be delivered by additional methods. Information and inspiration can now be shared through: CDs, conference calls, audio links, videos/DVDs, books, websites, seminars, webinars, and on-location training events. As long as certain fundamental pieces are intact, the form of delivery doesn't matter when the Result is successful duplication. Information, motivation, and opportunities for association with like-minded people are the ingredients needed to deliver consistent Results.

Successful NM companies became great because they figured out how to connect with their people, or connect their people to them. I do not mean by the methods they use, because all companies have access to the same methods. The great companies have effectively conveyed the importance of actual participation (Belief) in their System. Their distributors participate! They don't all make money, but the percentages work in their favor. This single factor gives these winning NM companies their success. It isn't their product or their compensation; it's their system. What makes the Amway, Pampered Chef, or Mary Kay even more victorious is the number of ex-distributors who speak of their wonderful experiences, lifelong friendships, and the personal development they acquired as distributors.

In October of 1988, I was sitting in a high school auditorium as a new distributor, for the second time with the same company, at a business-building seminar. The speaker was talking about a System, as he placed a toaster on the lectern. He put two slices of bread in the toaster, pushed the lever lowering the bread, and continued to speak. Every few seconds, he would glance at the toaster waiting for the bread to pop up—as toast. This went on for about a minute before someone in the audience yelled, "It's not plugged in!" The speaker pretended not to hear this cry, but then many others joined in. He continued to speak until everyone in the room clearly understood the lesson. A System must be in place, and you need to plug into it. If the System is good, your System Core Belief will always be increasing, and you will rarely question its importance or relevance. It will also become a key factor when discussing your opportunity with new distributors. You are going to invest two very important commodities in building your business: time and trust. Your Core Belief in the System will make a significant difference with both.

**Belief in Your Upline:** My son is in the Marines. A few years ago, I asked if the reason he was re-enlisting was because he liked it, and he replied, "No, there are good days and bad days, but we are all in it TOGETHER." This is what your upline can do for you. They create the synergy of a team. No matter what you are going through, you know you are not alone. Your upline, and the team of people who sponsored you, are available to help you. Believing in them provides you leaders to learn from, and examples to follow. Similar to my son's feeling of togetherness, you should hope to find (and develop) great relationships with people you can count on.

> ### DNA-*b*
>
> "When the student is ready, the teacher will appear."
> -Buddha

Core Belief in your upline can only be developed by spending time with them. Whether this connection is made over the phone or in person, the sooner you can do this, the faster you gain appreciation for what—and who—you have your hands on.

Building Belief in your upline is simple to do, if they are worthy. Alternatively, Belief in an upline who does not represent themselves properly is almost impossible. Worthy upline are people who, like you, are regularly plugged into the System. They should also be examples of the good things, which assist you in your journey. What they should NOT be expected to be is perfect. Your upline should be encouraging—whether directing you toward helpful information, or working directly with you. Your upline is not going to "do it for you." In reality, you should be looking for someone who will "do it with you."

You often make your upline better by following the System's recommendations. You give your upline more to work with if you use all of the resources and are doing the work. I have found if we ask the right questions, we can learn something from almost everyone and almost every experience. With regard to the people in your upline, ask yourself this:

- What do they do that I know I should be doing?

- What do they do to facilitate a positive response, and what causes a negative one?

I am hopeful your upline is good to you, but they can always be great training examples—good or bad. You will find the more you do properly, the more your upline will become available to you. Properly means you are following the System's directions but does not always mean you are succeeding. I can tell you from experience as an upline to many, I am always looking for those distributors who are working in union with the System. These are the people I invest in. I believe anyone who does enough of the right things will eventually make it. The opposite is also true. I believe those who don't apply themselves in a manner the System recommends usually end up failing. With time being such a precious commodity, working with those who don't follow the System is often an unwise investment of my time. Lastly, although Belief in your upline is terrific when you have it, you can successfully overcome not having Upline Core Belief.

A final thought—you are looking for relationship, inspiration, and honest constructive criticism from your upline. You may not find this in one single person and may need to look to different people for these. If you are not able to find each of these directly in your upline, then look cross-line to acquire what you need. If you are doing what is required to win, someone will always avail themselves to assist you.

**Belief in Your Sponsor:** Whatever your sponsor did to get you in front of the opportunity is all you should ever expect from him. He did something right, didn't he? If he is your friend, expect him to be your friend. If he is an associate from work, or friend from church, see him as that person, and expect nothing more. If you met him in line at Wal-Mart, then appreciate him for opening his mouth and showing the business to you. If he does anything else for you, consider it is a blessing. Nothing more should be expected, and if by chance you think he

> ### DNA-*b*
> Luke Skywalker:
> "What's in there?"
> Yoda: "Only what you
> take with you."
> —Characters from George
> Lucas, Star Wars Movies

is not all that sharp, he did get you to look. Your focus should be on becoming the best distributor ever sponsored, not your sponsor being the best in the world. This will ensure those you bless with the opportunity will never wonder whether they should believe in you.

**Belief in Yourself:** The problem isn't how we lack incredible Dreams, but rather, in most cases, how we failed and have been beat down so many times we often won't lift our heads to look up and see what is possible.

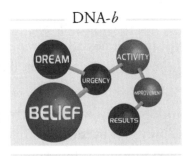

DNA-*b*

If you are part of the customary 20 percent of everyone who sets the goal, works the plan, and feasts at the victory table on a regular basis, you most likely have a strong sense of self and have an overflowing Self Core Belief. If you are the 80 percent, conversely, you probably regard the 20 percent as lucky, weird, and probably over-bearing. Even though you may think they are more capable, I would urge you to take a personal inventory. A close study may show your Dreams separate you from the achievers. You'll likely find your Self Belief may be setting your limits. Ouch!

How can some people succeed, and others fail, using the same system? My good friend Ryan Chamberlin, author of *Now You Know*, says, "It boils down to your personal characteristics—and the way you conduct your NM Activity." Simply said, you are the problem. Don't get mad at me. I didn't say it!

Did you hear anything about personal development during your company's opportunity presentation? I sure didn't at mine. So what does *personal development* have to do with network marketing? The answer is: EVERYTHING!

What could you accomplish if you knew you couldn't fail? I love this question, because it reminds me, and I suspect you, of what life could be. So why haven't we lived up to these possibilities? We have put limitations on our expectations, causing us to change our actions accordingly.

If I were a psychologist, we would now regress or go backwards, attempting to figure out why you have set limits on what you think is possible. However, I am not qualified to do this, but I *can* help you release these limitations.

The seven Core Beliefs we have covered previously, if dealt with properly, will positively affect your Self Belief limits and allow you to pursue your Dreams with Urgency. Everything you need to win is within your grasp. Want me to prove it to you? Extend your arm out, open up your hand, and turn your palm upward. Now, let me ask you a question. Do you have any music in your hand? You read the question right—do you have any music in your hand? Since the time I was born through August of 1992, my answer would have been, "No; I don't have any music in my hand!" I am guessing this is the same answer as yours.

### DNA-*b*

"Most people don't fail because they Dream too big and miss the mark; they fail because they Dream too small and hit it."

What changed that August day is subtle, but evident. It is simple, but answers a complex set of questions. How can the answer be "Yes?" What if I placed a radio in your hand (the first seven Core Beliefs) and turned it on (the eighth, Belief in Yourself)? Would you hear music? Was the music on before the radio was ready to play it? Of course it was. You just have to be prepared to *hear* it. Everything you can imagine is well within your grasp; you just have to be in a position to *receive* it.

The music in your life is all around you, but you have to be tuned into it. It never leaves you. You have to quiet the noise in your head and focus on a *new* music, which allows you to Dream and educates you to change. I don't know what the psychologists call it, but in NM, it is *personal development,* and it can inspire you to achieve anything you dare to Dream!

Success leaves clues, and the characteristics of those who are successful differ from the characteristics of those who are not. It's inherent, belonging by nature or habit. In a phrase, it could be "they think differently." In a word, it sure sounds like some sort of *DNA* to me. Albert Einstein said, "The definition of insanity is doing the same thing over and over again, and expecting different Results."[15] So, I say, "If nothing changes, nothing changes." For you to get more, you have to *become* more. Lucky for you, NM provides you all of the tools and examples to accomplish this. According to the DNA-*b model,* Results are accomplished after a chain of events, starting with the base pair of Dream and Belief. They have to be strong enough to support your journey to success, and this means you do, too.

# SECTION 2

# Urgency and Activity

*"First, decide what you want.*

*Second, determine the price you are going to have to pay to get what you want, and then resolve to pay that price."*

\- H.L. Hunt

## CHAPTER SEVEN

# URGENCY: Someday Never Comes

*"Without a sense of Urgency, desire loses its value."*

- Jim Rohn

URGENCY DOES NOT COME from a decision to be Urgent. The DNA of Business explains URGENCY as the natural by-product of an existing DREAM and a willing BELIEF. It isn't something you make happen; it is something you let happen. It isn't something you fight to change; it is something that fights to change you! It is natural. It is exciting. It is a "given," if your Dream and Belief elements are healthy. It's Urgency. If properly utilized, it can propel you to what you want in life; if left un-checked, it will surely leave you questioning why so many of your Dreams became unachievable.

Monday, Tuesday, Wednesday, Thursday, Friday, Saturday, Sunday, and someday—oops, I sneaked one in on you, didn't

I? Well, is it really that out of place? Most of us start working around age twenty and hope to retire around sixty. That means we have twenty-four hours a day for seven days a week in a fifty-two-week year, over a forty-year span. This totals 349,440 hours, and this is the number of hours you have to create your Dream lifestyle. How are you doing so far? Most people have an awakening somewhere along their time line that, although they have the *luxury* of deciding what to do with their time, they become consumed by their failure to obtain what they want. With almost 350,000 hours at our discretion, I am surprised at the most common excuse people give for not getting what they want: "I just never seem to have the time to do what I want to do!" How can this be the case?

My beautiful daughter, Kayla, was visiting me while I was writing this book. We were just leaving my place for a day of Golden craziness, when she asked me to stop at Starbucks. Being the "a lesson is in everything" kind of dad, I took the opportunity to relay a story I had heard from my friend, Steve, a short time back. The lesson for her was about handling money. For you, it is an analogy for what we do with our time. I inserted myself into his story to make my point to her. This is what I said . . .

I stopped by a Starbucks one day and had a caramel-apple-spice Grande, which set me back about four bucks.

Steve: *I hope that spice is really good.*

Me: *Yummy!*

Steve: *I mean it better be really, really good.*

Me: *What do you mean?*

Steve: *Eric, do you realize you just exchanged $4.00 for*

*a drink that took you just a few minutes to guzzle down?*

Me: I know. *What's your point?*

Steve: *I hope it was an incredible drink, 'cause you will never be able to use that $4.00 for anything else ever again.*

And then it hit me: we exchange our time in the same way, with no regard to what it means to us in the long run. We are so busy using our time today, we often have not invested it into the things that will take care of our wants and needs of *tomorrow*—and that is what I mean when I say, *someday* never comes.

### DNA-*b*

"There are no rollover minutes in life."

Pretty interesting stuff, huh? Here is the kicker—even though you now know this, the odds say most people will never do anything about it. This is the reason this chapter is so important. It helps you beat the odds. If you are reading this, you aren't looking for me to tell you only why we fail. You are looking for me to help you succeed. Your solution can be in understanding the role of Urgency, where it comes from, and how to manage it.

A friend and I were discussing the topic of Urgency. The question arose as to why people weren't more successful. "Is it a question of not knowing what you want, or is it not knowing how to get it?" Thinking people don't know what they want is ludicrous. From the earliest age, we want big, bright, beautiful, and tasty things. We want to feel rich in emotion with regard to the way we look, the way we feel, and the people we love. This is surely not the problem. Saying we don't know how to get what we want is a great excuse for failing to get it and is exactly what it is—an excuse! This is also not the problem.

If it isn't knowing what you want or knowing what to do, then, what is it? To borrow a commonly used phrase, "It's not rocket science." The answer is not *not knowing,* but it is *not doing!*

*Three frogs are sitting on a log, when two decide to jump off and swim to the river bank. How many frogs are left? The answer is three. Why? Because deciding to jump and actually jumping are two different things.*

Hey froggy, I know you can swim. Urgency is where Dream and Belief intersect. It is the point in your life where you know your Dream, you have Belief, and you are willing to jump. It's the feeling when you get the courage to walk up to the girl (or boy) at a dance and say, "Hi." Urgency propels you to risk being uncomfortable and doing the unusual when the goal is in the crosshairs, and you Believe the Dream is worth it.

DNA-*b*

Urgency has an enemy, and its name is habit. Our habits have delivered us the life we have today. Dreams are things you don't have. If you had them, then they would be reality, and habits would have delivered them. Therefore, in order to achieve and fulfill new Dreams, you need new habits. This is a simple sentence, but it is insanely important. For your sake, please read it again.

Just in case it didn't resonate the second time, I have taken the luxury of writing it again: Urgency has an enemy, and its name is habit. Our habits have delivered us the life we have today. Dreams are things you don't have. If you had them, then they would be reality, and habits would have delivered them. Therefore, in order to achieve and fulfill new Dreams, you need new habits.

Successful people have unique habits common among those who win. They know what they want (like you do), think about how to get it (like you do), and do what it takes (sorry, not this time). If habits are a major factor in getting what you want, then not having the specific habits to make your Dreams come true is keeping you from succeeding.

When Urgency propels us to do something new, habits throw us off. From the moment we wake up, we have programmed ourselves to do the same things and think the same way on a daily basis, like our morning cup of coffee from Starbucks. To go a step further, we even have habits about how we feel about things, not just how we think about things, causing us to constantly feel the same way about things every time we think about them. Financial problems— I'll get by. Relationship problems—Things could be worse. Health problems—If I can just get through the day . . . Do these sound familiar?

Urgency is the starting point to disrupt your daily routine. It is where you can emotionally fight with yourself. It is not an intellectual battle, but rather your conscious wanting to deal with your subconscious feelings. Urgency has to be big, and it has to be bold. It has to be significant enough to have a fighter's chance. In order to get what you want, it has to propel you to be better than the person you are today. Ever feel like you are bruised on the inside, emotionally? This is why.

Fighting to be more than we are is dangerous stuff! Conditioning ourselves over the years to accept who we are, our lot in life, and the fact we are doing OK makes life survivable, despite all the things about it we would like to change. It can even make it good. As nationally renowned author and speaker, Jim Collins, often says, "Good is the enemy of great." You want more? You need to do more—or maybe just differently. Everyone who wants more comes to this point of Urgency. To make the changes necessary, you will need to jump. For this, you will need an ally.

*Priority* is the fastest way to change the habits that, until now, have only gotten what you have—not what you eventually want. Billionaires in a group were once asked to write down their personal key to success. The only restriction was it needed to be legibly written on the back of a postage stamp. I am sure they paid homage to many great ideas that day, but the only one passed down to me was this one:

(1) Make a list.

(2) Prioritize the list.

(3) Do the list.

We are blessed to be living in a country with many freedoms. Our ability to decide what to do, when to do it, and with whom to do it, presents wonderful opportunity. So, given all of these choices, why do we often find ourselves struggling? Maybe having choices isn't the blessing, but making the right choices is?

Priority is defined as "the state of having the most importance or Urgency." I believe it is our understanding of *importance or Urgency* that may be the problem. As a society, we cater to what is *in our face,* rather than *our overall best interest.* This is not to say that, at times, these two can't be one in the same. When what is Urgent is also important, we have no problem prioritizing. Our difficulties can often occur when we are accommodating the Urgent, when the Urgent isn't really important in the long term. We concentrate on the unimportant Urgent because of habits. We will only have time for the truly important Urgent if we prioritize!

Although a parent doing things for his child, a purchase made to make us feel better, and an hour relaxing while checking Facebook or watching television, can be seen as both Urgent and important, the ramifications need to be examined.

What if you perform a chore your child was supposed to do? You think, "It's not worth the argument." Is this teaching life responsibility properly? What lesson is this for your child—and think of the habit you are forming in yourself? What if you spent all the money you made as it came in? Will you ever have money to purchase

> DNA-*b*
>
> "Our lives are a series of planned tasks interrupted by moments of awakening."

bigger ticket, or more important, items in the future? This lesson, not learned, can keep you from ever having the things you really want. Lastly, relaxing on the couch, at times, is necessary. Doing this when you *feel like it,* however, may develop a habit that keeps you from doing what is truly more important to you.

Our lives are a series of planned tasks interrupted by moments of awakening. Sometimes this changes our life's path, while other times, it is just a temporary blip in our heart rate. Urgency puts you in a state of mind where you are willing, and desiring, to make changes in your life. Habits must be disrupted, and priority must answer the bell.

I get the whole "Want more, do more, or be more" concept,

but maybe you don't yet believe it. The most successful people are not always busier than the rest of us. In fact, the opposite is often true. *Priorities* is not doing more; it is doing what is important. Priorities are often doing fewer things than you do today, but they must be the more important things. What

achievers do is leverage their choices into having a bigger effect. They do the tasks that provide the most return. This provides them the lifestyles that many want to mimic. The good news is you can do the same. It is this simple: Make a list. Prioritize the list. Do the list.

---

### DNA-*b*

"I have been impressed with the Urgency of doing. Knowing is not enough, we must do it. Being willing is not enough, we must do it."
— Leonardo da Vinci

---

Urgency puts you into what is commonly referred to as "the zone." Whether Michael Jordan is shooting a basketball, Bruce Springsteen is singing a song, or a mother is humming to her baby cradled in her arms, they are of single-minded purpose. This is what happens when *Dream and Belief* are tapped into. It isn't about you. It comes from within, and when you are Urgent, you don't allow others to interrupt your focus. It is as if you were born for it. You have no choices in your head, no concern for the Result, just a complete resolution (and satisfaction) that you are doing what you should be doing at that very moment in time.

Sustaining the Urgent element in network marketing can be tricky. Life does intrude, and negative people attempt to interrupt your concentration. In order to be most effective, you must sustain Urgency long enough to create good habits through the next element, Activity.

An important analogy can be drawn between maintaining Urgency and taking a road trip. Have you ever packed up the car, family, and dog to leave for vacation? What did you do when, at some point, you realized you forgot something? This happens to all of us—don't you just hate it? When this does happen, we go through a mental process that goes something like this: Do I really need it? Who should I yell at for forgetting it? How much time will we lose going back to get it? What will that do to our schedule? Repeat over and over.

DNA-*b*

When we start the Activity element in the DNA-*b* model, the Urgency element is required to get us far enough down the road so we won't wonder if we need it, won't look to blame someone for it, and most importantly, won't consider turning back! You will have drawn and stepped over the proverbial line in the sand.

Urgency is the *spark* to your action. For some, settling into proper habits, or Activity, can be accomplished quickly. For others, you will find yourselves back at Urgency a number of times. Let me assure you that each time you arrive back at the Dream/Belief intersection, you are given a new chance to *try it all over again*. Take the opportunity to reassess your priorities, draw a new line, and get back into the game as quickly as possible.

## CHAPTER EIGHT

# ACTIVITY: Game Time!

*"Just play. Have fun. Enjoy the game."*

- Michael Jordan

THE COMMON RESPONSE when asked why most people fail in network marketing is, "They don't do the work." Although many often don't do the work, your newfound knowledge of the DNA-*b* should provide you a different conclusion. You should now realize that "doing the work" should never be a problem for someone who has proper Urgency. In fact, it should be the natural response.

ACTIVITY, for the purpose of the DNA-*b,* means doing the work. It is taking enough action on a continuous basis to derive a response. Sometimes the response is positive, and sometime it is not. In both cases, you are moving forward according to the DNA-*b.* For the time being, consistent Activity will imprint new habits, while having a positive effect on your Belief and providing a training ground for your Improvement.

I have chosen to break up this explanation of Activity into two chapters. Originally, I had absolutely no good reason for doing this, other than my desire to keep the chapters in the book about the same size. When I went through the final editing process, I discovered a great reason to break them up. This first chapter deals with the Activity relating to the business presentation, and the next one takes it from there. Inviting people to look at your opportunity, and actually showing it to them are the two measurable Activities that will propel you through this Activity element and prepare you for Improvement.

If, as Lao-Tzu has said, "A Journey of 1,000 miles begins with a single step", wouldn't you want it to be in the right direction? A number of years after being introduced to NM for the first time, I was sponsored into a business by Terry McEwen, a person I never met before the presentation. I was a cold contact. Terry has since become a storied success in NM, and now a lifelong friend. What I want to share with you is his initial counsel, because it has led me to success on my own business journey.

### DNA-*b*

"The average person knows and keeps social contact with approximately 150 people. This does not count acquaintances."
— Robin Dunbar

Terry explained the importance of getting off to a good start. He said the steps are simple: Develop a list of 100 names, call all of them for a home meeting, and let the Results of that meeting speak for itself. Wanting to succeed, I did exactly what he told me. I am aware, though, most people will not, not because they can't—they just won't.

I don't mean to be critical, but I have told this specific story to hundreds of thousands of people (one-on-one, speeches, and in audio recordings), and most people still don't do it. But for you, since you invested your hard-earned cash for some help, I wish you would just do the 100 thing—it really does work!

Exposing your business opportunity to others is NM's primary Activity. The first requirement in doing this is making a list. Making a sizable list of prospects is critical to moving through the Activity element. A short list of names will not allow you to work consistently, or long enough, to gain Improvement. Not letting the numbers work on your behalf often leads to failure. When you have a long list of names, you greatly enhance your chances of succeeding.

Given the importance of this step in your journey, let me break down the big list theory even more. First, survey the list to gain greater confidence that many will likely find your business intriguing. Second, if any one person happens to decline

DNA-*b*

an invitation to join you, many others may still have interest. Third, a big list allows you time to Improve your contacting technique and confidence (increasing your Belief!). This, ultimately, makes all the difference.

A few key points that will greatly assist you in making a sizable list should not be taken lightly. As a professional earning an income in NM, you will want to teach this concept to others. Doing it correctly for yourself will allow you to understand what others may feel as they develop their own list of names. When making your list, understand you may never need to do it again—if done right the first time. List building isn't like mowing the lawn or cleaning the house. It's more like laying sod or building your home. Strong work at the beginning makes upkeep much easier.

Making a list properly will take a little time. I would give it at least a few hours. I only partially agree with many companies who are promoting getting your business started quickly by making a short list of your best ten to twenty names. This does spur a bit of excitement, but, in the long run, you will need to have a list of at least 100 to 200 names. If your list remains small (say, ten names), then two prospects who are not interested takes away 20 percent of your inventory. In contrast, if your list were 200, it would be a non-issue; two people could easily be brushed off. To develop a sizeable list, you can begin gathering names and numbers from your cell phone directory, Facebook and LinkedIn contacts, Christmas card lists, and any association or club membership rosters you have at your disposal. They are all fair game. By doing this, a couple hundred names isn't a stretch.

Now comes the pre-judging—most people's next issue. Perhaps you are concerned about what you'll say or what they'll think. For the purpose of making a list, these concerns are duly noted, but not relevant. Oh, they are concerns. I want

DNA-*b*

"Who are your best five to ten contacts? Let's meet 'em for coffee."
— Troy Brown

you to know I am aware you have them, and they need to be addressed. What I am asking you to do is just make a list of the people you know. What you will say to these people, or whether you will even call them (which you may not), need only be addressed after your list is built.

Many people in NM feel putting a name on a list is a commitment to call the person. It isn't. All it means is he is a living, breathing, person who would recognize you if you said, "Hello." It is really that simple. Putting 200 names and numbers on paper, with a cross-section of people with whom you could call, spells s-u-c-c-e-s-s.

This pre-judging thing is such a curse and debilitates you from what you are truly trying to accomplish. You don't pre-judge when recommending a restaurant, do you? Then why do it when you want to write someone's name? If your product is good, your contacts should want it. When building your list, don't focus on that yet. Just make a list!

If the thought of adding someone's name makes you feel automatically locked into calling them, consider using this logic: Does he eat? Would you recommend a restaurant? Now apply whatever you are marketing and use this format. Think along these lines: Does he want great health? I'll give him a recommendation. Could he enjoy traveling? I'll give him an option. Might he want or need more money? I may have the answer.

After you have developed a strong list, the next thing to do is to rank your prospects. You want to be in business with the most motivated and successful people you know. These are actually the people you might want to call first. This is often where the anxiety starts. Some think these people are *untouchable*. They call this the "Chicken List" for a reason. This anxiety can be relieved by having confidence in a number of factors. If you know what you are going to say, believe in your product, are prepared for certain responses, and you remember each prospect is only one name out of 200, you will have greater confidence. Until you have this confidence, focus your attention on contacting those on your list with whom you are more comfortable prospecting.

Doing something we are not confident in can bring a positive Result, but it most often leads to a more problematic Belief issue. Failing when you are not confident can be devastating. Prospects saying, "No" is part of the NM process, but it still isn't something you may ever get used to—or comfortable with. You may already be stepping out of your comfort zone to call people in the first place: be sure you know why you are doing it, and you believe your opportunity is one worth sharing.

---

### DNA-*b*

> "Most of your "No's" will mean nothing, but a few "Yeses" could mean EVERYTHING!"
>
> -Bert Gulick

---

As you move through the DNA-*b* model, you are systematically training your mind to a new way of thinking. Your Dream becomes more real because you now have a way to fulfill it. Your Belief becomes controllable because you know through perspective (information and evidence) you can change it. You learn to react only to Urgency, which is aligned with the things that are also important. Now, arriving at the Activity element, you should feel almost anything is possible.

As the two main components of DNA-*b* Activity, *inviting* and *presenting* carry with them a similar mindset and synergistic measurables. The mindset directs your side of the interaction between you and your prospect. In order to put your best foot forward, you will need to develop your posture. Posture, in the DNA-*b*, is defined as being in control of yourself through the entire sponsoring Activity experience. This is commonly referred to as, "Knowing that you know, that you know, and conveying this to others."

The synergy in the measurables between the number of people you consistently invite and the number of people you consistently show is downright mind-boggling. If posture is knowing you know, then consistently inviting and showing is printing the money. This is where two of my favorite business quotes intersect.

**Network Marketing:** *You have control over two things—How many times you show the plan, and to whom you show it.*

**Traditional Business:** *The best way to predict the future is to invent it. (Mavericks at Work* by Taylor and LaBarre, Foreword, 2006).

NM has a universally accepted method for contacting people, and I would be remiss without explaining it. Know it is, without a doubt, the simplest to learn and most duplicatable I have found. It can be adapted for any NM company, any product, any culture, and every demographic. For the life of me, I cannot figure out why some struggle with it, or say something else. Oh, wait a minute . . . I forgot. This is network marketing. That explains it; that explains everything. This is the world where people say, "You don't understand. My friends are different."

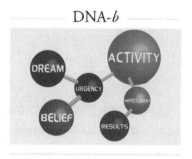

DNA-*b*

I know your friends are different. Your success usually boils down to you adapting to what works for the majority. You can bend it, build from it, and add to it, but this contact is best used in its raw form. So here is the most successful contacting method used by NM people all over the world:

A proper and effective invite has four basic parts:

(1) Be in a hurry.

(2) Clear the date and time.

(3) Show sincerity.

(4) Confirm the date.

This contact should only take about thirty to forty-five seconds, and it provides you natural posture if you do it correctly. You have permission to adjust, alter, and affect any of the parts to make yourself comfortable. With this said, I want you to know that altering it in any way won't (in most cases) make your prospect more comfortable. In fact, any alterations will most likely reduce the effectiveness of the invitation, while making it less duplicatable by others on your team. If you want to enhance, embellish, or encourage your prospect during the third part (showing sincerity), go ahead. What you should never do, however, is adjust the order of this contacting method. Be sure you go: (1) Be in a hurry by showing a sense of Urgency;

> ### DNA-*b*
>
> "We are what we repeatedly do. Excellence, then, is not an act, but a habit."
>
> -Aristotle

(2) Clear the date and time; (3) Show sincerity; and (4) Confirm the date.

Your single reason for contacting is to set a time to show your business to a prospect. If you were not in NM and you were calling a friend to meet you at a new restaurant you discovered, your conversation would look something like this:

(1) Hey, I only have a minute. (sense of Urgency)

(2) What are you doing for lunch tomorrow? (clear the date and time)

(3) I tried a new restaurant, and it's awesome. (show sincerity)

(4) OK, great. I'll meet you there at noon. (confirm the date)

Although your natural tendency might be to rave about the restaurant before step one and two, doing so will reduce the number of successful lunch invitations. This is where you are supposed to challenge me on this. I ask and recommend; you don't. Remember you bought this book to make money in NM. This invite will do it. Trust me!

When you get someone's voicemail, here is a proven message that works best, at least for me. You will not obtain a 100 percent response, but it delivers Results if they want or like talking with you.

> "Hi Paul, this is Eric. Hey, I have something important I want to run by you. Nothing is wrong, but it is important. Can you call me back today? My number is 352-555-XXXX. OK, Paul, get back to me as soon as you can."

Even if you are calling your brother or your best friend, be sure to say your name and your phone number as I did. It really works. If they like you, they will normally call you back fairly quickly. If they don't like you, I (seriously!) recommend you read *How to Win Friends & Influence People* by Dale Carnegie. This book will dramatically increase your chances of success!

When you begin contacting people, be prepared for a myriad of responses. They range from positive to negative and, if you're contacting properly, responses rarely have anything to do with what you are saying. Their reaction will have more to do with what they were in the middle of doing when you called, or, frankly, their habitual answer to all things. Included in their response might be what they think of you, and how busy they *think* they are. Using the contact I described will provide you ample Results and minimize, although not eliminate, the excuses—if you make enough calls! How many should be on your list? Just seeing if you are paying attention.

Whether you want to lead with your product or your income opportunity, consistently using the same contacting phrase will allow you to handle the questions that normally arise. If you use multiple invite phrases, you will have a great deal more to learn. Learning one invite properly is more efficient.

## CHAPTER NINE

# ACTIVITY: Expose Yourself

*"The man who has no problems is out of the game."*

- Elbert Hubbard

IF YOU WANT SUCCESS in network marketing, you are going to have to go public! Ask yourself this question. . . If you poll every one of your friends, will they say you are aggressively building your NM business? Let's be real for a moment. If *they* don't consider you Active, why do you think you are?

Showing your business opportunity to prospects is the second main component in the ACTIVITY Element. The DNA-*b* requires you to share the business consistently enough to gain real experience. Only while you are making presentations can the mechanics of what you are doing be IMPROVED for better RESULTS.

As you have read, you have control over two things: How many times you show the plan, and to whom you show it. Your phone calls will dictate to whom you show it, but your true NM experience will come from how many times you show the plan. After you gain experience and you have a chance for Improvement, you will mostly concern yourself with the number of people you actually sponsor. You can't sponsor them if you don't show them, and you certainly can't show them if you haven't called them. Seeing a theme yet? So we will focus, for the time being, on the number of exposures necessary to move down Success Road.

In order to succeed, you don't have a minimum number of exposures you need; however, a NM standard of fifteen exposures a month puts you in the game. Less than fifteen monthly exposures can provide you seating in the ball park and a chance at winning, but NM experts agree that the fifteen exposure mark is the magical sweet spot. Again, success is all about numbers. If you expose your business to fifteen people, and you sponsor the industry stated average of around 20 percent (or about three people), you will see a bit of growth in your group and have a chance one of the three actually doing something.

> ### DNA-*b*
>
> "The Activity Element is when the rubber meets the road. Burn it up!"
> -Me

Fifteen exposures generally means you are consistently investing time making calls, and therefore, developing a bit of a flow and confidence with that part of your business. People usually don't quit something they are confident in doing. Your action provides a dual benefit: You're getting better, and you're getting Results. Less than fifteen exposures in a month is still building, but it is like occasionally playing basketball on week-ends—you're not going to get much better, and you are likely to cramp up, or even hurt yourself, before the game is over.

I mentioned the average sponsoring rate is about 20 percent. If your credibility and/or likeability are high, you may find better Results. If these are in question, you might sponsor fewer. No matter whom you are, the networking effect from your Activity takes some time to grow. From the moment you consistently call everyone on your list and show your business plan at least fifteen times per month, things will still take four to six weeks to get moving in the right direction. You may require an-

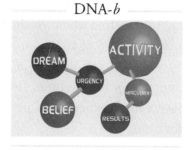

DNA-*b*

other four to six weeks to see the group size and dynamics begin to change, but you will definitely feel it.

Important Note: If you are making calls, but people aren't returning your call or committing to an appointment, you may be low on the likability/credibility scale. I realize people are very busy and they may not have called you back for various reasons. My intent isn't to offend you, but you may need to consider the *possibility* that you may greatly benefit from reading the Carnegie book I mentioned earlier. Ask your upline for additional recommendations to assist you, and then take what you learn to heart! For the time being, you may want to ask your sponsor to call the people on your list. This is not the best scenario, but it could be your best option.

As in *Contacting* and *Inviting*, some universally accepted practices need to be ascribed when showing the plan. Back in the day, I had to personally meet with my prospects to share my opportunity. Today, a significant number of presentations are done on or over the computer. Although both of these methods have been proven successful, you need to know you will sponsor at least two to three times the number of people when you meet them face to face. Don't work the computer because it is more convenient. Pay your dues, and watch the money come back tenfold as your business grows significantly faster!

If you are in proximity to your prospect, you can share your business through a large local meeting held at a hotel or office, a home meeting where you invite many people to one showing, or one-on-one or two-on-one presentation meetings. Each of them works, and they are all better than doing one over the computer or on a website. These provide you an opportunity to have a more experienced person with you to meet your prospect, too.

Even if you are the one doing the presentation, a second NM person from your company can play the role of the expert. Having a third party answer questions, offer a testimony, and even ask for the sale, can be extremely beneficial. With this said, the third party does not necessarily have to be present. Someone is always a phone call away if you need assistance. Note: The NM definition of an expert is when you tell someone this person is an expert. However, this person is almost always someone in your upline who, in fact, has more experience and expertise than you. Voilà, an expert!

DNA-*b*

"Your network will always build slower than you thought it would, but always bigger than you ever thought it could."

When you are unable to get with a prospect personally (local scheduling conflicts or the prospect lives out of town), you can do a person-to-person web presentation or webinar, or you can show him/her a video presentation found on your company's website. Because the webinar has more of the personal touch, it will provide a better Result.

Did I convey how I highly recommend personal presentations versus sending them a video (aka computer dating)? In person meetings allow you to interact with your prospects. I believe in personal presentations, because sending people to the web doesn't allow you to be in control of the timing. This often Results in a waste of your time and may cause you to lose a good prospect.

Don't get me wrong. I have sponsored hundreds and hundreds of people over the years after they viewed an online presentation. The time waster is the people you send to a website who then become elusive afterward. You know the feeling. "What happened to Charlie? He said he was going to look at it today and call me. I left one message, and he didn't call me back. Did he even look at the thing? I am going to call him again, but I don't want him to think I am pushy. Okay, this is ridiculous. I have left 34 messages, and texted 119 times, and he still hasn't called me back. I know he would be incredible at this thing, if he would just call me back!"

When you *allow* someone to do something when they get to it, you are, in essence, allowing them to control the flow of information. This is very dangerous to do. It not only takes you out of the driver's seat, but, as described above, makes you appear to be chasing them. The roads are littered with millions of former NM people who decided letting other people control their destiny was easier and better. I am not saying you should be demanding, belligerent, or a jerk about it. What I am saying is learn how to direct people to view your information at a specific time so you can remain in control of the process, effectively answer questions, and move the process along.

In the case where you have some short presentations or teaser commercials, you could say something like this: "Hi Aunt Brenda, I'm glad I caught you. Look, I only have a minute . . . are you gonna be at home tonight around 7:00?" If she says yes: "Great, I have something important to run by you when I have a little more time. I'll call you right around 7:00 then." At that point, I don't even say good-bye. I don't consider this rude, but you may. If you do, then say "good-bye."

When I call back at 7:00 p.m., I tell Aunt Brenda I am glad we had a chance to connect because I have something important she needs to see. I ask her to go to a computer, and while she is walking, I tell her why I am excited. If she is going to watch a short teaser, I stay on the phone while she watches it. When the video is done, I ask if she likes what she saw, and if she would like to know more. If she does want more, I can direct her to a full presentation at this time. Then I schedule a time to get back with her and, only then, give her instructions to the next video.

> ## DNA-*b*
>
> "You still use a shotgun approach, but use a sniper rifle."
>
> -Me

What we say regarding our excitement is essential, but it should only be a confirmation that what a prospect is about to see is really important to us and we want them to give it a good look. I don't recommend giving the details of the presentation at this stage. Remember to always try to stay in control of the flow of information nicely, but with posture.

Before the action is requested, always clear a time first—got it? If someone is interested but doesn't have more time, schedule a follow-up call. This type of appointment is the most effective way of sharing an online presentation. You know when it begins, ends, and you are available to answer questions immediately. We are not perfect, and we don't live in a perfect world, but we can attempt do it the best way possible.

I have to go back to something I wrote earlier. I know I have hit this repeatedly, but it is imperative. Always try to get in front of your prospect, rather than do something over the phone on the web. You will need to become a better inviter, but your success will dramatically Improve. I know the number of exposures may go down, but it will be worth the trade.

The final step in Activity is the follow up procedure. The follow up is best done immediately after the conclusion of the actual presentation. Over the years, I have learned that those who walk away, normally stay away. You may think your company's product, price point, or system, makes a one-stop

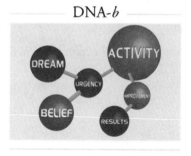

DNA-*b*

close out of the question. I will tell you the DNA-*b* says you are wrong. Some caution: People can have legitimate reasons for having to think about it. They may want to test the product, talk with their spouse, or wait until they get paid. What you need to know is these are ALL excuses that, over time, an Improved you will learn how to overcome. You will also come to appreciate how getting a "Yes" at the end of a presentation is addictive—and duplicable!

Okay, breathe for a moment. Those who have made money in NM will accept what I have offered more comfortably than those who are still awaiting their first four-figure month. No matter who you are or how many successful years in NM you have had, I know you agree learning how to overcome objections can only be done by overcoming objections. This is as vital to your success as oxygen is to your body.

Here are a few helpful views that have worked for me:

*"Only those who risk going too far can possibly find out how far they can go."*

- T.S Eliot

*"Your motivation must be absolutely compelling in order to overcome the obstacles that will invariably come in your way."*

- Les Brown

*"We would accomplish many more things if we did not think of them as impossible."*

- Vince Lombardi

A great number of experts have written volumes in the field of salesmanship. The great ones, Ziglar, Hopkins, and Rohn, will have you develop your selling technique from a sincere Belief that you are truly assisting the person to whom

> ### DNA-*b*
>
> "The purpose of a leader is to get someone to do something they want to do, but wouldn't do it without you."
> — Tim Foley

you are presenting your business plan. Other experts, often self-proclaimed, will teach you methods to engage in verbal jousting that surrounds the sale. Whomever you mimic, the learned skill is not helping them out of their problem or out of their money. The key is learning when your prospect wants to say "yes" and may need your support. Network marketing is a real business, and success comes from helping others when they don't know how to help themselves.

Consider the following points as the framework for leading your prospect to the "Yes" you want him to verbalize:

- Ask him to get in. The single biggest reason people don't close the sale is they don't ask for the order. The world will not end if your prospect declines. Just think of the numbers that would have said yes if you would simply have said, "Let's go ahead and start?"

- You should always get a verbal form of commitment before asking him to buy. This can be done with questions like: "Can you see the benefits of . . . ?" "Can you think of a few friends who would . . . ?"

- A few of my favorites: "Would you be comfortable being paid for referrals of friends and associates who bought this?" "Are you the only one on your block who would find this valuable?"

- The verbal jousters say get your prospect to say "yes" three times to something before you ask them to purchase.

- Some people effectively use, "Any reason why you wouldn't want to get started?" I find this increases your prospects comfort level in asking questions and lowers his barriers.

- Even after a rejection, ask your prospect to get started at least three times before you consider moving on. You have to learn how to handle this, because you do not want to come across as uncaring about his initial negative response. Find out why, overcome it, then ask again.

## CHAPTER TEN

# ACTIVITY: The 5-Minute Bank Account
## *The Set Up*

THE 5-MINUTE BANK ACCOUNT METHOD WORKS! No substitute for experience exists, and, in a very short period of time the 5-Minute Bank Account provides you just that. What you will learn with regard to contacting and inviting will forever affect your Results in a positive way. With this said, you must know in advance that, although this method will require LESS time than you would normally invest, most people will disregard it because it seems too simple. Don't make this mistake!

Successful business people find ways to leverage their money to produce more income. The majority of people who join the NM industry do not think they have any money to leverage.

This lack of available finances is often the primary reason for getting started in the first place. However, many choose this industry to leverage another precious commodity—their time.

The single most crucial trait of a successful NM person is the ability to invite. You need to become a professional inviter. Since this is THE most important facet of success in NM, then avoiding it either delays your success or dooms you to failure. I would like to introduce you to a method for inviting I have followed for many years. It has created significant incomes for many people because of its design. It takes away the "I don't have time" excuse and provides a compounding effect vital to your NM success. It requires a single 5-minute interval each day, multiplies it over the week, and compounds it through the group you are building. It is that simple.

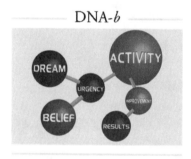

DNA-*b*

By investing five minutes a day calling prospects, your appointments will compound into producing consistent growth and increasing profit. My observation is nearly all who create the 5-minute habit of making calls see a four figure per month income within about ninety days. The Results may vary depending on your company's compensation plan, but this duplicatable method will develop the kind of residuals you are seeking—a residual income with a lasting downline Actively working their businesses.

You must be wondering what you can really accomplish in just five minutes. If you went into the gym and did a 5-minute upper body workout every day for thirty, sixty, and ninety days, you would not be ready for a wrestling match, but you would see and feel a difference. If you wanted to learn how to play the guitar and practiced five minutes every single day for the same periods of time, you may not be ready for a concert, but you would be measurably advanced. Consistent practice creates IMPROVEMENTS and RESULTS. This is the key—doing a short, doable amount of work over a long enough period of time to see Results. Making daily calls produces appointments, which ultimately generate presentations and sales. The 5-minute method I am explaining is the crutch you can use to balance and establish the successful habit you and your group are seeking.

Someone got rich by producing a video tape called *Eight-Minute Abs*. Why don't you make a fortune on the 5-Minute Bank Account? Everybody has five minutes. The biggest challenges you will face are agreeing five minutes can produce enough momentum to develop a viable income and believing in your ability to create the 5-minute habit.

"Making real money has to take more than five minutes a day," you say. The method itself is only five minutes a day. You will put additional time into your business, but it will not feel like the specific 5-minute interval. You won't find it difficult at all.

A friend of yours hears you started a new venture and asks you what it is. Will you have a problem getting together, or will you make the time? No matter how packed your schedule, you will happily make room to give a presentation. The time problem seems to be no problem when we have a willing prospect. Having a time problem usually refers to having trouble prioritizing call scheduling over other things. Once you create a 5-minute habit to make your calls, your business can progress aggressively.

Success in NM is all about the contacting. Now that you understand this, you have to get good at it, and that requires repetition. If you go to the gym once a week, do you get in better shape? No. You hurt yourself. If you play the guitar, and only pick it up once a week, are you any better? No. Your fingers hurt, and you get frustrated. Consistency is essential.

Success isn't only about who you are, but also what you do. I speak from experience, not because I am special, but because I found success by applying these principles. If you implement the 5-Minute Bank Account, you will create the habit to put yourself in front of enough prospects to grow your business successfully and create cash flow. Once success begins, your Belief level increases, while those who you sponsor can duplicate your same 5-minute effort.

## CHAPTER ELEVEN

# ACTIVITY: The 5-Minute Bank Account
## *The Daily Ritual*

THE 5-MINUTE BANK ACCOUNT starts, as everything does, with the Dream. With many NM plans, this method will create income in the next few months and significantly more over the course of a year. What will you do with the money? Additionally, how good will you feel having large numbers of people in your team who are also working consistently and achieving their Dreams?

Do you believe everyone has five minutes to make a few calls? I know we are all busy, but a whopping five minutes? Yes, you need a clear head and to be focused when you make calls—but five minutes? Five minutes is only 300 seconds, less time than it takes to do a zillion other things you do every day. Would you agree it isn't the length of time (five minutes), but creating the habit that is the problem?

### *First Rule:* Make 5-minutes of phone calls, to set appointments, before you eat lunch.

You have to prioritize (URGENCY) the five minutes. To ensure your calls are made, I suggest you anchor the thought of making calls to a *daily* task you are already doing that is important to you. Do you eat lunch? Most of us usually set aside a period during the day where we take a break (even a short one) and eat something. My suggestion is to take five minutes before your first bite of lunch, and make your calls. I have found this much more reliable than writing make calls on a to-do list. Do you use the bathroom at work? Make the calls while you're in the bathroom. Do you get a break at work? If so, make calls.

Avoid making calls when you get home. First, things are c-r-a-z-y when you get home, and you can't normally be consistent. Second, the people you are trying to reach are going through their own personal chaos at their house. Finally, you will most likely not be able to meet them that night, so everything gets delayed by a day. If possible, always attempt to block out your five minutes during the day. If you think calling them somehow infringes upon their normal business, remember most people don't love what they are doing and may find your call a convenient break.

The Activity is making five calls during five minutes. Experts say a habit takes twenty-one days to create, so do it for at least twenty-one days. I encourage you to make a commitment for thirty days or a full month. By the way, calling the same five people doesn't count! Thirty days would require about 100 names—that list you made a few chapters back, remember?

If you start with a list of 100 people, you will have enough different names to last the entire month. You won't get through the entire month without clearly seeing a difference in your business—and *feeling* a difference in yourself. Making five calls each day creates enough Activity for you to get really good at the contacting and inviting part of NM. You'll find yourself contacting people outside of your five minutes just because you have become so confident. It's contagious! The commercial is correct: a body in motion, *stays* in motion.

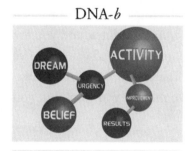

DNA-*b*

A trick that will help you is to purchase a package of 3 x 5 index cards from the store. Any type or color will do. Write five names and numbers on twenty of the cards. Don't worry about what order you group the names—you'll be calling them all this month. You only need twenty cards, because on day twenty-one, you will go back through your cards starting again with day one. You are thirty days down the road, and you have actually called 100 people. Think something will be different? You know it will.

## *Second Rule:* Make a list of five names and numbers, on a new index card, each night before you go to bed.

Be sure you have five names and numbers on tomorrow's card for the next day's calls. I suggest listing them out before you go to bed each night. DO NOT wait until the morning—you will have too many things to do at the beginning of your day. If you do it the night before you go to bed, you will have something to look forward to the next day.

Then, after waking up, take the card everywhere you go, until you make your calls—all five of them.

This next point will make you happy. You don't have to actually talk to the five people on your index card. You only have to make the call. In today's busy world, most of the calls you make will end up going to voicemail. What makes this method so appealing is you can count voicemails as one of your calls. Do I hear yippee out there? The call counts just the same as it would if they answered. Five calls in five minutes, and you are done for the day. If you make five phone calls, and you leave five messages, get this: You are done! That's your day. Congratulations. No more calls. You can make more if you want, but you don't have to.

**Special guidelines:**

- You can't make ten calls on Monday and then no calls on Tuesday. You can make as many as you want on Monday (at least five), but you still need to invest five minutes for five calls on Tuesday.

- If you actually speak to someone and set up an appointment or two for that day, you can stop making calls on that day. You don't have to call all five if you were successful with the first two. By the way, if you set appointments, and they call you back to cancel, you're still done for that day—yeah!

## CHAPTER TWELVE

# ACTIVITY: The 5-Minute Bank Account
## *Fishing Leads to Catching*

I LOVE TO FISH. When I am fishing for large-mouth bass, my favorite lure happens to be an artificial, red shad worm. I catch more bass on red shad worms than anything else. Some of my friends who are good fisherman tell me to use colors like watermelon red, pumpkin seed, or even cotton candy. Now, I am sure they catch many fish on those variations, but I don't. I don't, because I don't use them. I don't have any confidence in them, so I don't use them. I do catch a ton on red shad. Red shad is the best. I tell everyone to use red shad. By the way, my friends catch an equal amount on their colors of choice, too. I guess any good approach works if you do it enough. You see, inviting people to look at your business is very much like fishing. Pick a phrase, catch some fish, gain confidence, and have a feast.

Now that you will be making close to 100 calls over the next thirty days, you need to have something to say. You need a contacting phrase that makes you feel confident. The phrase you use will change over time based on the experiences you encounter. I gave you a four-part invite in chapter 8, which is a great place to start. Many people find they are actually saying too much in an effort to set up an appointment. With regard to inviting, the less you say, the more curious your prospects are, and the more likely they will want to meet with.

In a way, you are looking for the people who are looking for you. You're not looking to sell someone the opportunity. You're looking for the person who *wants* to look at the opportunity. If they respond positively to a good inviting phrase, then you have proven to be someone they know, like, and trust. You are not able to earn those characteristics on a thirty-second phone call. What you do not want to do is say things that get in the way. This isn't about you; stick to a script that shows your Posture. Your opportunity is exciting, and prospects will want to see it. After you tell them you are in a hurry, and clear the date for an appointment, you can say, "Something came across my desk, and I thought of you." If they ask what it is, tell them that is why you set the time you have already cleared. If they ask more questions, remind them you are in a hurry, and let them know you'll tell them everything when you meet.

If you feel using a curiosity contact seems like you are misleading your prospect, I want you to know I understand how you feel. I felt the same way. What I found is I was not able to convey the magnitude of my product or my program over the phone. Getting into a discussion usually led to failure, because prospects kept asking questions, and often they concluded their interest based on limited information. Isn't providing a poor substitute for the presentation over the phone misleading, especially if you believe in the importance of properly showing them? You may not think you are doing your prospect (and yourself) a disservice by explaining things over the phone—but you are!

If you get someone's voicemail, use this approach (using their name, of course):

*"Hi Dan, this is Eric. Hey, I have something important I want to run by you. Nothing is wrong, but it is important. Call me back. My number is . . ."*

I even leave my own brother my phone number, know why? Habit. It's my routine, and I am creating a habit. If I get out of my routine even with my brother, then I may get thrown off on the next call. The following message works tremendously with people who know you well. They think, "If he left his phone number, it must be important."

*"Hey, Jeff, it's Eric. Real quick, you need to get a hold of me. I've got something important to talk to you about. Nothing is wrong, but it is important that I talk to you today. Call me back. Here's my number . . . " Click.*

When Jeff calls back, I say, "Hey, Man, look, I'm in a hurry. I'm glad you got a hold of me. Nothing is wrong, but I do need to talk to you tonight. Are you going to be home? I'm going to swing by. I can't get something *really interesting* off my mind."

## *Third Rule:* Create an effective contacting phrase that follows the four-part format.

You will encounter many different responses when you make your calls. Some of these have to do with what you are saying, but subconsciously, your prospect will combine what he hears you saying with what he thinks of you as a person. If you have strong credibility, you can get away with saying more things than if your prospect questions your morals, ethics, or experience. This need not deter you from making the calls. It should only alter the contacting phrase you are using.

You have to think of yourself as ten-feet tall and bullet proof. Remember, some NBA players are under six-feet tall, but you don't often see them driving to the basket trying to score.

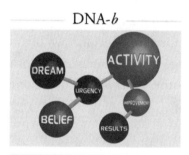

DNA-*b*

Whether you are nineteen and have no real business experience, or you are forty-five and have failed in every network you have ever tried, means little, if you handle yourself properly.

A few years ago, my brother and I were talking about why people don't return phone calls. He made a very awakening comment. He said, "Maybe they don't call back because they don't want to talk to you." Since he is my older brother, and an M.I.T. and Harvard graduate, I will take his word for it. I don't like it, but it makes sense to me. Some of the reasons people respond to you in the way they do is because you are who *you* are. Just because you think they should be in a hurry to speak with you doesn't mean *they* think they should. This is all part of the contacting process, so become a professional inviter and face the music. Your Dreams are right around the corner.

You have to put enough prospects through the system to have the odds working for you. You may be fortunate. Your first prospect agrees to meet you for a presentation, says "yes," and becomes your company superstar. You have to know the odds are against that, but hey, we can Dream! Commit to thirty *whole* days!

If you have a busy schedule, you will need to note the times when you can actually set appointments. Clearing an appointment time at the beginning of the contact phrase allows you to see if you want to go all the way through it and if your prospect is free. Ideally, you should try to set an appointment for the day you are making the call. If you aren't able to meet that day, try for some time in the next 24 to 48 hours. Attempting to meet quickly is important. It shows Urgency. It goes along with the in a hurry and got something important to run by you thing. When making calls on a Monday, your goal is to present to them on Monday. If you happen to have a home meeting on Tuesday, and you're making calls on Monday, feel free to target Tuesday. In this case, you are trying to create a bigger turnout.

If you are not able to set an appointment because your prospect is unavailable for the time you ask, you can either give him one alternative time or say, "No problem. I wanted to run something by you, but I will call you back in a few days. Gotta run." When you are new at contacting, talking about time availability without your prospect starting to question you can be difficult. You should never be afraid of using the "Gotta run, I'll get back with you in a few days" remark. After all, you have to make your five phone calls in five minutes, so you can't spend all of your time on one call. This creates a greater sense of Urgency.

Everything I have learned over the last thirty years about contacting and inviting, you will learn over a thirty-day period by doing the 5-Minute Bank Account. You cannot help but get good at something you do every day for thirty days. You surely will become a professional inviter with a 5-minute habit if you are consistent. Don't give yourself the luxury of missing even one day. If you miss just one day, missing the next one is that much easier—just like working out or eating healthy. If, tonight, you don't eat as healthy as you've been eating, tomorrow is harder to get back on track. An alcoholic cannot give himself the luxury of one drink, because he exchanges his new-found good habit for the old bad habit. We're talking about only five calls in five minutes for thirty days. It's do-able, and it works!

When I present my 5-Minute Bank Account at seminars, I am often asked how long it really takes to gain the "posture" I exude. This question makes me both flattered and frustrated at the same time. My ego accepts the flattery, and I think, "I don't expect most people to be able to contact the way I contact." I just don't. I've been doing it for thirty years, and I'm pretty darn good at it. But the reason I'm so good at it is because I have made dozens and dozens and dozens and dozens . . . and dozens of calls to prospects.

Getting good can happen really quickly. I get frustrated trying to convey this. By the time you speak to 100 people in a relatively short time frame, you will have more than 80 percent of the confidence I have gained over thirty years, and 80 percent goes a long way!

When I contact people, they know I have something that may be *special*. It isn't about what I say; it's about the way I say it. Your sponsoring success will be far greater if they are "feeling you" from your first point of contact. I wish I had a better phrase, but I think you know what I mean. When your child comes home, and you know he did something good (or bad) in school because it is written all over his face. It is *that* feeling. You're not losing people because they saw the presentation, and they don't get it. You are often getting "no's" because they didn't feel it from the very beginning. When they feel you're onto something—they'll want to know what it is. Nobody wants to be left out of something that could be big, and just wait until the light bulb goes on. Here is an example of what I mean:

I was giving a 5-Minute Bank Account training session to a few hundred people in Nashville, when Jonathan walked up to me and asked if I would come to a meeting and teach some of the people who weren't at the seminar. I accepted his invitation and met with twelve people from his group the next day. As I concluded my presentation, I asked what the people liked about what I had just shared. The overriding comment was the simplicity of five minutes a day. As I was getting ready to leave, I said to them, "How many minutes a day?" They answered, "Five." I said how many calls?" and they said, "Five!" Jonathan, all of a sudden, grabs my arm. His jaw drops all the way down, and he says, "Oh, my Gosh. I get it." I asked him what did he get? He said, "These twelve people are all in my group. When each of these people make five calls, that's sixty contacts every day. That's 400 contacts in a week! My group is going to explode!"

Let's re-cap:

- Make your list.

- Write the five names each night.

- Call the five names each day.

- Show your business to those who will set an appointment with you.

- Duplicate this within your group.

- Make a ton of cash and retire early!

# SECTION 3

# Improvements and Results

*"Seek first to understand, then to be understood."*

- Stephen Covey

## CHAPTER THIRTEEN

# IMPROVEMENT:
# New Year's Day

*"Never mistake Activity for achievement."*

- John Wooden

TODAY IS THE FIRST DAY of the New Year. I am not using this as a metaphor. As I write this chapter, it really is New Years Day, 2012. I knew when I went to bed last night that the new morning, the new day, and the new year was going to bring with it 300 million Americans who had set some sort of goal for IMPROVEMENT. When I woke up still lying in bed (I have always wanted to write that), the thought came to me: the reason almost every one of the 300 million will fail in their resolutions is because Improvement cannot be initiated until you go through the previous DNA elements we have been discussing, until the DNA-*b* model is followed. It really isn't just the DNA of Business at all; it is actually the DNA of every successful thing we do.

Ten Common New Year's Resolutions:

 (1) Spend more time with family

 (2) Start exercising

 (3) Eat better

 (4) Quit smoking

 (5) Enjoy life more

 (6) Quit drinking

 (7) Get out of debt

 (8) Learn something new

 (9) Help others

 (10) Get organized

Do they look familiar? I know January 1st is the day we try to commit to a number of these. How many times through the years have you reset a goal to do the things on this list? The reason you cannot complete the task is you haven't followed the DNA of Success process. Each of these resolutions is a Dream, but we skip over Belief, rush to Urgency, stagger through Activity, and get frustrated when we, or others, don't see immediate Improvement. We then begin to believe we are not going to achieve our goals, and we give up. The Belief element cannot be ignored, and you are missing a properly structured Improvement element that you didn't even know existed. You were destined to fail before you even began. We discussed the Belief element in chapters 3, 4, and 5. Fear can be a formidable opponent, and we convert to Belief if we want a chance at succeeding. With respect to the structure of Improvement, we will explain what it is and why it is important in this chapter.

Early in this book, you learned that base pair #1 was made up of Dream and Belief. Dream is a *positive* element, and Belief is considered more *negative*. They have a good cop-bad cop relationship. Base pair #2 is Activity and Improvement. They are both *positive*, and they have a rookie cop-veteran cop relationship. Only when Dream and Belief work together, with the rookie bringing enthusiasm and action, while the veteran imparts wisdom and caution, will they survive the shift. If they don't work together, you better believe somebody (your Dream) is gonna die.

DNA-*b*

The Improvement element provides a steady flow of nutrients to your Activity using three components: association, coaching, and positive relationships. Each of these is critical to maximizing your effort and pushing you through to RESULTS. Improvement will be easy if you arrive here with a Dream, have equal Belief, and are Actively in pursuit.

Your NM company and field leaders provide numerous opportunities to gather as a group. These may be highly structured events or more casual affairs. Any time you have a group-like experience, it is *Association*. The importance of Association cannot be overstated. It provides you so many nourishing things—tangible and intangible.

Association at meetings (a home or a hotel), trainings, team calls, and social potlucks provide tremendous reinforcement to all of the DNA-*b* elements. At an Opportunity presentation, you can watch a leader share your business with others. This can re-touch your Dream, fortify your Belief, and accelerate your training. It can also remind you of the priorities (Urgency) that are important to you. You will learn techniques at trainings to accelerate your sponsoring rate, while injecting life in your Dream and Belief. Even a potluck at a distributor's home or a holiday party can infuse a much needed dose of Urgency to move ahead.

National events hold a special place in the hierarchy of association. The importance of you attending is second to none. To understand why, you need only to look at one statistic. Almost 100 percent of the people who quit their company do so within 90 days of missing a national event. I could spend hours—yes hours—telling you why you should go. Since you have read a hundred pages or so from me already, I would rather boil it down to two thoughts: *Have you found a better way to get what you want, or have you decided you don't want it anymore?*

You CAN build a network marketing business that fulfills all your Dreams and goals. If you want more, you can have more, but you have to do more (or do it differently) and often *be* more. People at your company are making money right now. They are at the national meetings with the purpose of meeting you. They may not know you, and they may not even shake your hand when you are there, but your attendance in the room provides you every chance of success. You are proving this through your willingness to attend.

Over my career in NM, I have witnessed almost every excuse for missing an event. In each instance—every single one—the person missing the event did not come back as a rock star the next year. It just doesn't happen.

This chapter is about *Improvement*. This means I am laying it on the line for those who have graduated from Dream, Belief, Urgency, and Activity. This is not the reasoning, tone, or verbiage I would use for those still trying to figure out who they are and why they are here. If you haven't gotten to the Improvement phase, the event is all about gaining vision and confidence. Those who are in Improvement need to associate with others who are doing the work. The number of people in your local town who are in the Activity phase is nothing compared to associating with those whom you can benefit from on a national scale.

> ## DNA-*b*
>
> **"The Characteristics of a Leader are the abilities to instantaneously transmit Dream and Belief to the Listener."**
>
> —David Pietsch

Coaching is the second component of Improvement, and it is simply described as learning from people who are more experienced and have a vested interest in helping you succeed. Your coaching comes from having access to those qualified to coach. Coaching picks up where your company's training system leaves off. The system provides a complete education through CDs, videos, books, training calls, and events. Someone upline will direct you toward key instruction found in these materials. If you have learned this educational material and are following the steps through the DNA-*b*, you need a true coach. Finding a coach when you are in the Improvement stage is never a problem. Finding someone to invest a lot of time with you while you are still finding your way through the DNA-*b* model is another.

If you are not consistently Active, you don't need a coach. You need a Dream and/or Belief. Most company's systems are sufficient for you if you aren't through the Activity requirements (consistently exposing prospects). Because I want you to have some coaching tips, I added recommendations for the most prevalent issues you might encounter at the end of this chapter.

If you are consistently Active, your coach's job is to assist you in seeing things from another's perspective. Sometimes the Improvement is in the mechanics you use, and other times, it is more people-skill related.

This coaching interaction should never be a relationship based on superiority with status, position, or ego getting in the way. The coach should simply help you see what aspects of your Business, or the building blocks of your Business, could be Improved, and then suggest ways to meet those needs and challenges.

When you are being coached, you are responsible for sharing your true Activities and the areas where you feel you are having difficulties. You need to respect your coach's time and be mentally present and interactive when your coach is working with you. Taking direction and putting it quickly to use is necessary to see the Improvement you seek. If you don't accept guidance or put it to use, your coach will become less interested in supporting you. Good coaches do not waste their time; they work with those who listen, learn, and then proceed to fulfill the Activity phase of the business. Ultimately, you MUST be coachable.

As a coach, you are responsible for figuring out ways to assist others in obtaining Results. Sometimes you will need to spend time building the Business with the person you are coaching. Other times, you may be able to work out issues by just talking through situations over the phone. Regardless, you must remain available to the needs of your student.

A coach's role needs to be one of complete business integrity. Similar to a counselor, you need to be honest with him or her. Some people, especially people whose lives or egos are fragile, can be devastated if you are directly honest with them about their shortcomings. A good

DNA-*b*

"You either need to change your friends, or you need to change your friends."

coach uncovers their shortcomings, so they can discover how to overcome them. Essentially, the best thing for someone, especially someone who may come to the business with significant personal issues, is not to dwell on those issues, but simply to steer them to resources that may help him.

Positive relationships are the third component of Improvement. If association is time with the right people in your company, positive relationships is beneficial time with people outside of your Business. When I discuss this in my training sessions, this section always invokes really weird looks from people in the audience—like I am telling you who to spend time with and who to ignore. Oh, wait a minute . . . this is *exactly* what I am doing. This is only, of course, if you want to succeed in NM—or anything else for that manner. You will raise and lower yourself by the things you put in your head and the people with whom you spend time. But aren't these the same thing?

For the most part, the people with whom you spend time are people with whom you have been raised, people you see at work, or other family members. In each case, they are a given. What I mean by this is that they have given you enough positive encouragement and negative conflict to put you where you are today. Make no mistake about it—they are a huge influence on your lifestyle. Please don't fight me on this. I am in a book, and I can't fight back! If, by chance, you think I am wrong, let me prove it to you (not the part about me being in a book, but the part about your friends' influence).

Think of the four people you hang around the most:

(1) Do they positively encourage you?

(2) Are they people whose advice you seek and follow regularly?

(3) Would you want them to be your NM sponsor?

(4) If you could somehow meet them today for the first time, would they likely become one of the four people you would hang around with the most over the next year?

We have good friends, and we have people who are good for us. They are often the same. In the case where they aren't the same and you find yourself feeling restricted to move ahead, new friends could be a good thing. Sometimes, this is all you need to be freed from your current restrictions. As you begin to succeed, some of the people who were restricting you may begin to recognize the changes in you. Who knows? Your example may become a positive influence in their life, too!

As promised, here are some coaching tips. They are intended for people involved in NM who want to cover the basics. They certainly will not provide you all of what you need, but they will expose you to some areas you may need to Improve. Put them to use.

- Obtaining Success: Do the work. I often say, "If you want to go W.O.W.—you need to *Work on Working!*" Nothing replaces face-to-face interaction on a consistent basis.

- Getting Started: Create, or steal from this book, a contacting phrase, and call your best five prospects in the first 24 to 48 hours. Then call your best ten in the first week. A good goal is to sponsor someone in the first three days and three in the first week.

- Booking Appointments: Conversation before presentation always leads to failure. A professional inviter learns to say the least to get the most. This is not evasive; it is sincerely the best way to have a prospect see your presentation the way it was intended—without pre-judging it.

- Booking Appointments (if you have a poor NM history):

Most of the people joining a NM business today have failed in previous NM programs. Hiding your past from the people who know you is as problematic as highlighting it. Using a straightforward, four-part invite is best here. Be prepared to answer for your past with something such as, "Like Edison and the light bulb, I have found a number of things that didn't work. I have paid my dues around this industry. I believe this one is different. Will you spend a few minutes with me so I can tell you why?"

- Booking Appointments Trouble (PROCEED WITH CAUTION – SENSITIVE TOPIC): If you cannot get people to return your calls, or take a look at your program, you are probably very low on the likability or respect scale, or you just may be leaving the wrong voicemail message. Chances are that it has nothing to do with the company you are in or

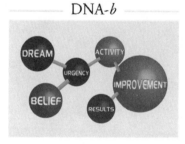

DNA-*b*

the presentation you would like to show. It is because of your personal DNA, your make-up, your personality, and possibly your people history. When you find yourself with this issue, figure out what about you is so detrimental. Admitting or hearing this can be difficult, but it isn't impossible to analyze. Just ask your family or your close friends. They will tell you why you lack credibility. You can then work to change it while you are cold contacting new prospects. If this is your problem, be sure to use a classic four-part invite and get very good at clearing the date.

- Exposing the Business: The best way for you to show a presentation is by using the company's or upline's recommended materials. Your part in the presentation is to get a prospect to look at it, show sincere interest in what is being explained, and learn how to tell your NM story. For example, "Let me tell you what happened to me when I saw this thing ... "

- Finding Someone in Your Group Who Will Do Something: You are in your group. Are you doing all the things necessary to be successful? If you are, you will have new people join, and they will have a great example. Then it won't matter if the members of your current group are or are not doing everything that they should do.

- Finding Someone in Your Home Who Believes in Your Ability to Succeed in NM: Ask them for their support for 90 days. Then, get to work!

## CHAPTER FOURTEEN

# RESULTS:
# Alice in Wonderland Meets the Wizard of Oz

*"As we look ahead…, leaders will be those who empower others."*

- Bill Gates

I MUST WARN YOU. This last chapter may have a tad bit of sarcasm. You probably aren't surprised, but I want to clarify this, just in case you aren't sure.

I have narrated the DNA-*b* training more times than I can count. The model has been scribbled with crayon on a restaurant's tablecloth, fingered into the sand on an international beach, etched into snow with my ski pole riding a lift, and shared from a stage in conferences from Jersey to Japan. No matter my experience in presenting this model, I was ill-prepared to put it on paper when I began to write.

To say this was a work-in-progress would be inaccurate. The content was sound, and the message was clear. My problem was the writing itself. The words wouldn't come through my fingers as I hunted and pecked at the keyboard. I could verbally explain it to a Rhodes Scholar, but, on paper, it came across like a kindergartner's first watercolor. And then it hit me: *follow the model.*

I, too, had to adapt my own DNA to the DNA-*b*. I found a way to take who I brought to the dance and produce the RESULTS I was looking for, but I still struggled. I had to progress one element at a time, as I clarified my DREAM, fortified my Belief, prioritized my Urgency, and consistently did the Activity, while being coached to Improvement. You see, I am not only the author of the DNA-*b*; I am also a subscriber.

This final chapter is written in two parts. The first includes the three most important lessons I know to share. The second will provide specific instruction about when to apply these three lessons. Your newfound knowledge of the DNA-*b* can propel you to the NM successes you have desired. You will need to transition this knowledge to experience and your experience to instruction. To reach these life-changing heights, you not only need to be a working example, you must also coach others successfully.

---

### DNA-*b*

"You can have everything you want in life, if you help enough other people get what they want."
– Zig Ziglar

---

You no longer have to watch the people on your team fail to achieve even the lowest levels of NM success. You now have an understanding that transcends this flawed reality. You understand the problem isn't their lack of effort or consistency, and it's not because they don't have time or can't face rejection. We have a lot of ground to cover, and with just one short chapter left to send you on your way. Let's Make It Happen . . . together!

# PART 1

The DNA-*b* is a model for networking success. It is not only your personal guide, but also your gauge to figure out where you and others are stranded. Most people in NM are evaluated by their success. Did they hit this level, get this bonus, or qualify for this trip? This is a fair method if you are ranking people, but what purpose does this serve if your goal is to help them succeed? It does provide a quick evaluation of what they have done, but you should be far more interested in what you can do to move them along.

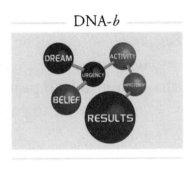

DNA-*b*

A favorite NM quote comes from the Lewis Carroll novel, *Alice's Adventures in Wonderland*. It is often echoed to extol the virtue of knowing what you want:

> One day Alice came to a fork in the road and saw a Cheshire cat in a tree.
>
> Alice: *"Would you tell me, please, which way I ought to go from here?"*
>
> Cheshire cat: *"That depends a good deal on where you want to get to."*
>
> Alice: *"I don't much care where."*
>
> Cheshire cat: *"Then it doesn't matter which way you go."*

What if I told you knowing what you want would allow you to move in the right direction? I know you agree with this and understand the importance of the Dream.

However, do you realize any attempt to get someone to go to work consistently before they know what they want is futile?

## Lesson #1—You will be better served learning how to help others identify their wants and desires than you will by repeatedly asking them to bring someone to your house meeting.

### DNA-*b*

Professional inviters make money, but professionals in NM learn how to lead people, and make a fortune!

You're thinking too much; make things easier on yourself. You want something, think you can get it, and begin to doubt you can do it. You then decide it is not worth going after in the first place. I know you think I am over simplifying this. But, am I? This is the mind's process, and you can't ignore it.

If you want to know whether you really can build a NM business, honestly answer these questions:

- Do you have a Bucket List of some things you want in life? Are you are willing to accept criticism from some people who may not admit they, also, want these things?

- Are you willing to invest time to get what you want? Do you believe waiting for the perfect time will mean it will never happen? Are you willing to lose some sleep to get what you want?

- To get where you want, would you follow the yellow brick road if the Wizard, himself, gave you a map to his castle? Will you carry others with strange deficiencies— no heart, no brain, and no courage—with you? When a cackling, short witch hurls fireballs at you, and flying monkeys steal your dog, will you still be interested?

- If you have questions, are you willing to use life-lines to make sure you don't go home without any money? With an unlimited number of opportunities to phone a friend, will you take their advice?

These are the only questions that matter, and they are not far from NM reality. You have now answered them—good or bad. This business, industry, and world are plastered with people who Dream. What you need to know is the world is controlled by the people who believe. Do you just Dream, or do you also believe?

## *Lesson #2*—Begin as a good example. Let your leadership emanate from this humble beginning.

When evaluating the leaders who have built large organizations, no one personality type monopolizes the list. They come in all shapes and sizes, with backgrounds so varied it would make the United Nations look like The Mormon Tabernacle Choir. They are just like you. They all had a reason to start and were willing to begin where they were. They waded through the muck and the jellyfish to keep surfing until they found that perfect wave.

Some people come with traits, experiences, and situations that make building a NM easier. Others have more difficulty. They took what they had and added what they needed to get what they wanted. So, why can't you? Top NM income earners have the ability to help other people share in their Dream and buy into their Belief. Although each of these leaders go through different learning and growing processes, they all can strap their groups on their back and fly them to places where anything is possible and everyone is invincible.

Some have an innate characteristic, while others pick it up it along the way. Leaders are not always the best looking, best speaking, or the best _____ (you fill in the blank). They are *connectors*. They put you emotionally in touch with the things you want so badly you can taste them. What is most interesting is those who never make it in NM seem to lack this leadership characteristic, and they seem unwilling to develop it.

"People want leadership . . . and in the absence of genuine leadership, they'll listen to anyone who steps up to the microphone. They're so thirsty for it they'll crawl through the desert toward a mirage, and when they discover there's no water, they'll drink the sand. People don't drink the sand because they're thirsty. They drink the sand because they don't know the difference." (*The American President*, directed by Rob Reiner in 1995).

### *Lesson #3*—Until you learn Lesson #1 and Lesson #2, let someone else lead your group. They won't follow you anywhere anyway.

## PART 2

You now understand the DNA-*b* model as described throughout this book. Two elements are at the beginning (Dream and Belief), and one is at the end (Results). You have invested a few dollars and a couple of hours reading through my book and now understand what each element individually represents. Together, they represent the DNA-*b*. By fortifying one element, you are automatically propelled toward the next element, ultimately buying your freedom.

You already knew success in NM can only happen by helping others do the same. For this reason, I have made a last addition to the DNA-*b* diagram. I call it "drawing a line in the sand, and this time I am being metaphorical.

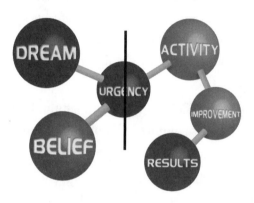

Part 1 of this chapter explained the importance of learning the lessons to assist people left of the line. Unfortunately, most of the people you encounter in your business will remain left of the line and never get to real Urgency. Learn to use what you have discovered to become the type of person who moves people to act. Everyone left of the line is in need of strengthening their reasons for building their business and in need of increasing their confidence that they can. You will not accomplish this by teaching them methods to sponsor others. You can only move them along by teaching them methods to re-sponsor themselves. Many will not follow your lead, but those who do will be indebted to your example for the rest of their lives. This is where motivation is truly inspiration, and great leaders have proven enough inspiration can change the course and enhance the lives of great numbers of people.

The DNA-*b* model is suited to handle the single most difficult aspect in building a large group—knowing when someone actually crosses the line. However, you have to be able to *identify* that they have actually crossed it before knowing what to do.

If your goal is to help your people move along the model, figure out where each person is at any given time. This is accomplished in quite an unusual manner. You do it working backwards. You evaluate where people are by looking at the model from the end (Results) towards the beginning (Dream and Belief). Practice doing this by finding yourself first. Where's Waldo?

- Are you self-sufficient and getting all the Results you can handle? If no, then move left to Improvement.

- Are you trying to Improve through counseling because you are encountering new situations from consistently sharing your Business? If no, then move left to Activity.

- Are you Actively exposing the opportunity through presentations, at least 15 times per month? (Hey, I would take 10 to12). If no, then move to Urgency.

- Are you Urgently prioritizing your schedule to make the time necessary to share the opportunity on a weekly basis? If no, then you are left of the line.

- Do you have a Dream you are not willing to do without? Most likely you do, so look at what is left.

- It's a Belief issue. Bingo! Welcome to the real world! You win the prize. The reason people don't succeed in network marketing starts and ends with their ability to believe they can, and more importantly, they do. Those Core Beliefs will get you every time. I could have written this on the back cover, but I wanted you to buy the book. It's more valuable because I've buried it—like treasure! That's your prize!

B-E-L-I-E-F spells trouble, if you don't have it. If Belief were a body part, it would be the liver. You can't live without it, and you don't ever want it to become an issue. When it works properly, it filters out all the bad stuff; when it doesn't, you are sick. Belief is the single source of your biggest conflicts in everything you do in your life.

The key to success has more to do with your Belief than anything else. If knowledge is power, think of yourself as all-powerful. This is how you use your power for the greater good. You now know more about the DNA-$b$ than anyone you are advising. After evaluating where someone is on the model, you can enlighten him to move on. Most people will require a good dose of Dream or Belief therapy.

If someone can't cross the line, you should focus your counsel on the importance of the first two elements. If he does get past Urgency to Activity, you can teach him how to teach it to others. Only through helping others possess or capture a Dream and Belief will you ever be truly fulfilled.

# Endnotes

1. http://en.wikipedia.org/wiki/%C3%96tzi_the_Iceman

2. http://ezinearticles.com/?Einstein---Definition-of-Insanity&id=12047

3. http://ghr.nlm.nih.gov/handbook/basics/dna

4. *Microsoft Encarta College Dictionary,* 1st ed., s.v. "belief".

5. Direct Selling Association Facebook Page: http://www.facebook.com/permalink.php?story_fbid=10150549311582180&id=91555322179

6. The Trump Network, Pampered Chef

7. Amway Forever-http://books.google.com/books?id=VXNuZED4ibMC&pg=PP18&lpg=PP18&dq=amway+distributors+gerald+ford&source=bl&ots=wLYuYeEvbP&sig=B6SERaP52bTHMZNI8AoWvxTKOP8&hl=en&sa=X&ei=dM82T7m5EsWosAL08dioAg&sqi=2&ved=0CEcQ6AEwAQ#v=onepage&q=amway%20distributors%20gerald%20ford&f=false

8. http://www.blogtalkradio.com/wealthysistas/2011/11/14/wealthy-sistas-top-mlm-women-onyx-coale-and-donna-allen-1

9. Robert T. Kiyosaki, *The Business of the 21st Century,* (Bhopal: Manjul Publishing House, 2012)

10. Wall Street Journal, June 24, 2011

11. http://www.dsa.org

12. http://www.directselling411.com/glossary-and-faq/industry-faq/

13. http://www.directselling411.com/glossary-and-faq/industry-faq/

14. http://www.directselling411.com/glossary-and-faq/industry-faq/

15. http://ezinearticles.com/?Einstein---Definition-of-Insanity&id=12047